Nationalism

Short Histories of Big Ideas Series List

Published

Capitalism By Paul Bowles

Feminism By June Hannam

Environmentalism By David Peterson del Mar

Communism By Mark Sandle

Nationalism By Richard Bosworth

Terrorism By Rosemary O'Kane

Available soon

Fascism By Martin Blinkhorn

Zionism By David Engel

Modernism By Robin Walz

Colonialism By Norrie Macqueen

Nationalism

R.J.B. BOSWORTH

PEARSON
Longman

Harlow, England • London • New York • Boston • San Francisco • Toronto
Sydney • Tokyo • Singapore • Hong Kong • Seoul • Taipei • New Delhi
Cape Town • Madrid • Mexico City • Amsterdam • Munich • Paris • Milan

PEARSON EDUCATION LIMITED

Edinburgh Gate
Harlow CM20 2JE
United Kingdom
Tel: +44 (0)1279 623623
Fax: +44 (0)1279 431059
Website: www.pearsoned.co.uk

First edition published in Great Britain in 2007

© Pearson Education Limited 2007

The right of Richard Bosworth to be identified as author of this work has been
asserted by him in accordance with the Copyright, Designs and Patents Act 1988.

ISBN: 978-0-582-50602-2

British Library Cataloguing in Publication Data
A CIP catalogue record for this book can be obtained from the British Library

Library of Congress Cataloging in Publication Data
Bosworth, R. J. B.
    Nationalism a critical history / by R.J.B. Bosworth. — 1st ed.
        p. cm. — (Short histories of big ideas)
    Includes bibliographical references and index.
    ISBN 978-0-582-50602-2
    1. Nationalism—History. I. Title.

JC311.B6633 2007
350.54—dc22

2006052478

10 9 8 7 6 5 4 3 2 1
11 10 09 08 07

Set by 35 in 9/15pt Iowan
Printed and bound in Malaysia

The publisher's policy is to use paper manufactured from sustainable forests.

For Sophia

Contents

Preface   ix
Series editor's preface   xiii
Timeline   xvi

Introduction   1

Chapter 1   Nationalism: strengths and contradictions,
                truths and lies   10

Chapter 2   Nationalism before nations; nations
                before nationalism   36

Chapter 3   Nation, nationalism and revolution
                1789–1914   63

Chapter 4   Imperial, national, racial and world war,
                1914–45   99

Chapter 5   International Marxism and the nation   131

Chapter 6   Minorities old and new, and the
                nation since 1945   167

Short bibliography   209
Index   212

Preface

My own nature is a rational and civic one; I have a city, and
I have a country; as Marcus I have Rome, and as a human being
I have the universe; and consequently, what is beneficial to these
communities is the sole good for me.

Marcus Aurelius, *Meditations*
(1964, Harmondsworth: Penguin), p. 101.

IN MOST WAYS, I am an odd person to write yet another account
of nations and nationalism. My practice of history has been
confined largely to exploring the political and social past of Italians,
most often during the first half of the twentieth century. I have
done so while pursuing a lengthy academic career, the majority
of it in my native Australia. It is true that I have displayed a
constant, if wry, interest in the discipline of history and in its
functioning both within the ivory tower and, for example, among
the memory-mongers in the so-called 'Italian community' in
Australia. But I am not a historian of ideas and am particularly
unconvinced by those historians who want to lock ideas and
theory away from their use and misuse, application and mis-
application, understanding and misunderstanding, by human
beings. I am also only too aware that plenty of historians with

more 'span' than I have already written about the history of the nation and done so with brilliant analytical skill.

Another book about nationalism – can it be justified? I have to confess to my readers and to my publishers that I am not sure. Yet, time does move on. The breakthrough historical accounts of the nation were written a generation ago in the 1980s, that decade when globalization was flexing its muscles and communism was fraying. Then the Berlin Wall had not fallen (nor had the Israel National Wall been built) and market 'reform' was still in its infancy. Twenty years ago, neither terror nor collateral damage was as much part of our everyday vocabulary as they are today. So, how does the idea of the nation, the theory and practice of nationalism, the credo that we belong to our national community, the requirement that human empathy be above all nationalized, seem in the new millennium? Why, in our times, do the nations continue to rage so furiously together? And what is the effect of their raging?

Gordon Martel, the series editor, kindly invited me to write this book quite a few years ago. I am grateful to him for the initial invitation and for the patience that followed during my tardy delivery. My thanks to the Pearson editorial team and especially to Christina Wipf Perry, Natasha Dupont and Colette Holden for the care they have taken with the book's editing and production. I am similarly happy to have pursued my life as a historian of this little book while at home at the civilized University of Western Australia and while 'playing away' at Oxford, at Reading and at various places in Italy. My own identity remains, I suppose, in some part, Australian (although I have been known to urge that 40 years of research on Italian history gives me some claim also to being Italian). But mostly I do my best to deny a national heritage in preference to my personal and family story, my global ventures and my hope of being a rootless cosmopolitan. I am a historian who tries to avoid being too tied to one past. This necessarily uncertain national identity may colour the pages about the nation that follow. I carry my national passport and pay my national taxes but I do not clench my fist on my heart when I hear my national anthem played. Rather, I treasure a lapel badge that combines the stars from the Australian national flag with an Italian tricolour in the left upper corner, where it substitutes the ordinary Union flag. If only, I sometimes sigh, nations were accepted as inevitable for the foreseeable future, which perhaps they are, we could all be permitted postmodern flags. Each would have a national base – in my case, the Southern Cross of Australia. But the other bit would be detachable and each of us could choose our moments of being partially Italian or Iranian or Chadian or American. Then, maybe, we could be individual, local, national and universal, without one factor overwhelming the other three, and so celebrate our national citizenship critically and disbelieve the nation's history as eagerly as we believe it.

My thanks to my world-ranging set of academic friends, especially in the case of this book to Graham White, Michael Ondaatje, Giuseppe Finaldi, Mark Edele, Gordon Martel, Roger Absalom and Carol Jefferson-Davies for their careful and important critiques. As ever I could not be without Mike, Edmund, Mary and the rest, including my newest grandchild, Sophia Anna Bosworth-Gerbino, half-Italian, half-Australian, half-New Zealander, half-American, half-Japanese and half-British, and so an infant reminder that 0.5×6 sometimes $= 1$.

R.J.B. Bosworth

Series editor's preface

WHAT MAKES THE WORLD MOVE? Great men? Irresistible forces? Catastrophic events?

When listening to the morning news on the radio, reading our daily newspapers, following debates on the Internet, watching evening television, all of these possibilities – and more – are offered as explanations of the troubles that beset the world in the Middle East, the 'war on terror' in Iraq and Afghanistan, environmental disasters at Chernobyl and New Orleans, and genocide in Sudan and Rwanda.

Where should we look to find answers to the puzzles of the present? To psychology? To economics? To sociology? To political science? To philosophy? Each of these disciplines offers insights into the personalities and the subterranean forces that propel the events that change the world, and within each of these disciplines there are experts who dissect current affairs on the foundation of these insights.

But all of these events, these problems, and even these disciplines themselves have one thing in common: they have a history. And it is through an understanding of the history of those ideas that inspired the people behind the events, and the ideas behind the ideologies that attempted to explain and control the forces around them that we can comprehend the perplexing and confusing world of the present day.

'Short Histories of Big Ideas' aims to provide readers with clear, concise and readable explanations of those ideas that were instrumental in shaping the twentieth century and that continue to shape – and reshape – the present. Everyone who attempts to follow the events of today via newspapers, television, radio and the Internet cannot help but see or hear references to 'capitalism', 'communism', 'feminism', 'environmentalism', 'nationalism', 'colonialism' and many other 'isms'. And, while most of us probably believe that we have a basic understanding of what these terms mean, we are probably much less certain about who it was that coined, invented or defined them. Even more murky is our understanding of how these concepts moved from an idea to become an ideology and, perhaps, a phenomenon that changed the world. Most bewildering may be the disputes and controversies between factions and divisions within the movements and political parties that claim to be the true followers and the legitimate heirs of those who first conceived of the concepts to which they claim to adhere.

The authors of these Short Histories have been asked to write accessible, jargon-free prose with the goal of making comprehensible to the intelligent, interested but non-expert reader these highly complicated concepts. In each instance the approach taken is chronological, as each author attempts to explain the origins of these ideas, to describe the people who created them and then to follow the twisting path they followed from conception to the present. Each author in the series is an expert in the field, with a mastery of the literature on the subject – and a desire to convey to readers the knowledge and the understanding that the research of specialist scholars has produced, but which is normally inaccessible to those not engaged in studying these subjects in an academic environment.

The work of specialists often seems remote, obscure, even pedantic, to the non-specialist, but the authors in this series are committed to the goal of bringing the insights and understanding of specialists to a wider public, to concerned citizens and general readers who wish to go beyond today's headlines and form a more comprehensive and meaningful picture of today's world.

Gordon Martel

Timeline

1707	Scotland merged into Great Britain
1776–83	American 'war of independence'
1784–91	J. Herder publishes *Reflections on the Philosophy of the History of Mankind*
1789–1815	French revolutionary and Napoleonic era destroys established map of Europe
1801	Inauguration of United Kingdom of Great Britain and Ireland
1805–72	Genoese Giuseppe Mazzini, philosopher of nationalism (and always unsuccessful practitioner of Italian 'revolution')
1810–26	Latin American states break free from Spanish empire
1822	Brazil separates from Portuguese empire
1828	Greece bcecomes an independent nation; Belgium independent
1845	Religious civil war in Switzerland
1848	K. Marx and F. Engels, *Manifesto of the Communist Party* sketches (Eurocentric) internationalism; revolutions in many continental European cities for 'liberty' and the nation
1849	Switzerland acquires modern constitution
1861	Italy becomes a nation state
1864	Foundation of International Red Cross
1868	Meiji restoration makes Japan a modern nation state
1870	Germany becomes a nation state
1874	International Postal Union founded

1878	Congress of Berlin recognizes Serbia, Bulgaria and Romania as independent nations
1889	Socialist 'International' established
1899	First Hague conference for international peace and law
1905	Norway becomes an independent nation
1907	Second Hague conference
1908	'National' Revolution in Turkey
1910–45	Japanese annexation of Korea
1911	Chinese revolution overthrows last of Manchu dynasty
1912	Albania uneasily independent
1914–18	First World War: great conflict of the nations?
1917	Bolshevik (internationalist?) revolution in Russia
1919	Peace treaties make independent nations of Czechoslovakia, Hungary, Austria, Estonia, Latvia and Lithuania, restore independence to Finland and Poland, and entail many other territorial adjustments in Europe and in the European empires. 'League of Nations' established in Geneva to preserve peace between the nations. 'Mandates' replace German and Ottoman rule in their empires
1921	Qajar dynasty overthrown in 'Persia'; talk of an Iranian nation
1922	Benito Mussolini becomes Fascist prime minister of Italy (extreme nationalism to power); Egypt independent but still under British guidance; 'Irish Free State' (called Eire from 1937) separates from Northern Ireland
1931	Japan invades Manchuria
1933	Adolf Hitler, chancellor of Germany, merging nation and 'race'
1935–36	Independent Ethiopia destroyed and annexed by Italy in last major example of European imperialism in Africa
1939	Slovakia made independent from Czechs as clerical-fascist German puppet; Albania absorbed into Italian empire; Ribbentrop–Molotov pact destroys independence of Baltic states and Poland. Outbreak of European segment of Second World War

1941	German destruction of Yugoslavia (Croatia independent) and Greece; invasion of the USSR. Japan seeks overthrow of white empires in Asia-Pacific
1945	After defeat of Nazi-fascist version of the racial nation, United Nations established in New York to preserve international peace. End of Italian Empire
1946	Philippine Republic independent
1947	India, Pakistan and Burma become independent states
1948	Israel becomes independent nation. 'Ceylon', later Sri Lanka, independent. North and South Korea have separate governments
1950 onwards	Accelerating decolonization of British, French, Dutch, Belgian, Portuguese and Spanish empires and creation of the myriad of nation states of Africa and Asia-Pacific
1971	Bangladesh independent state
1979	'Islamic revolution' in Iran overthrows the Shah to establish 'Islamic Republic'
1989 onwards	Fall of Berlin Wall leads to collapse of USSR, break-up of Russian empire and Yugoslav union and establishment of numerous successor nation states. Re-unification of Germany
1997	Establishment of parliaments for Scotland and Wales
2003	USA and 'coalition of the willing' invade Iraq, creating doubts about its survival as a 'nation'

Introduction

'FABRICATING HISTORY is an act of intellectual vandalism that poisons modern understandings of past misdeeds and heroism alike.'[1] So a leader writer in *The Economist*, cherished organ of liberal capitalism, concluded when faced with the Holocaust denial of David Irving. But the story of the Nazi Judaeocide is not the only segment of the past that can be subjected to crass manipulation or outright lies. Rather, as shall be seen only too often in the text that follows, the relationship between historical truth and the nation is fraught with difficulty. The nation, now in the twenty-first century close to being the universal political form – 'failed states', current rhetoric regularly tells us, need to enhance their 'nation building' – is almost always portrayed as finding its justification in a long, maybe 'age-old', past. Yet the idea of the nation is probably new. Certainly, national claims to seamless antiquity can be relied on to be false.

Here is one conundrum. There are plenty of others. During the past two centuries, the nation has been constructed on the practical programme that it will defend its citizens from enemy invasion and, within the national borders, enhance prosperity and ensure justice for all. As the expression of popular sovereignty, nations possess armies and tax collectors to enforce and pay for their rule. They are underpinned by legal and political systems that may share quite a lot with others but will always have some idiosyncratic cast. But these practical matters, where the nations have generally seemed successful in an era where world trade, world income, world population and the number of nations have rocketed upwards, are not the end of the story. The nation always boasts a metaphysical side; its 'meaning' is regularly said to lie in its control of time and space. A nation asserts its special relationship with a certain territory, one that is habitually sacralized as 'ours', even as 'our perpetual mother'. This sacralization of the land in turn prompts the view that a nation is made through the mystical fusing of its soil (and sometimes its flora and fauna) with the 'blood' of the humankind that has inhabited and developed it. Despite the triumph of the industrial and computer revolutions, nations continue to privilege agrarian origins and 'roots' (and to winnow agricultural subsidies slowly or not at all). In nations, city people grow misty-eyed at the national virtue of the countryside.

> *A nation asserts its special relationship with a certain territory, one that is habitually sacralized as 'ours'*

This religious sense of belonging to a land is seconded by a claim to eternity, indulged in by all nations. The acceptance of the national identity carries the religious promise that individuals are not only individuals but rather that they connect with their fellows across time through common membership of the nation. By being 'us', 'we' master death and, through our national fellowship, permanently draw its sting.

Here, then, the professional historian may gag, since the claims to own space and to patrol time are palpably false. No person in even the tiniest nation state can actually know every other citizen, while in nations of 100 or 1000 million and more, the idea is ludicrous in the extreme. Furthermore, all possess class, gender, age and other characteristics that tie them to people in other nations. Each person belongs to more than one potential 'imagined community'[2] and the nation's borders are too narrow for every individual sensibility. Equally, no single man or woman can identify with all nature in any state, however small; the idea is especially farcical in so vast a country as is my own place of birth and citizenship, Australia. No Australian has ever or will ever commune with every piece of the soil, flora and fauna of our continent. In sum, the metaphysical foundations of the gospel of the nation are absurd and false. Even a moment's thought about them ought to prompt a critical, 'anti-clerical', intellectual response to national religiosity.

The metaphysical foundations of the gospel of the nation are absurd and false

Contemporary developments over the past decade and a half make this conclusion still more mandatory. Since the collapse of the USSR and the withering away of its scheme, however incredible, of an alternative economy and culture to that of victorious liberal and nationalist capitalism, the uneasy relationship between the quotidian side of national existence and its claims to embody something greater have increased in tension. Economists and bankers may have proclaimed that they have

Benedict Anderson

Benedict Anderson is probably the most influential student of the nation over the past generation. The title of his main book, *Imagined Communities: Reflection on the Origins and Spread of Nationalism* (1983 (rev. ed. 1991), London: Verso) has become a truism.

Not easily categorized through national belonging, Anderson was born in 1936 in Kumming, in the Yunnan province of China, to a missionary family, some of whose members had been involved in the Irish nationalist movement. By 1941, the family had moved to California, where Anderson was educated. As an immigrant to the USA, Anderson retained Irish citizenship, a matter he deemed of sufficient significance to place on the title page of the first edition of *Imagined Communities*.

Anderson was a resident of Indonesia during the brutal 'nationalist' and murderously anti-Chinese coup of 1965. After his expulsion from Jakarta, and then spending time in Thailand, by 1983 Anderson, back in the USA, was seeking a better world than that created by US, Soviet and Chinese policy in Asia. Nationalism, Anderson argued, was a matter that needed to be set into the story of imperialism and its discontents. As he sketched the rise and triumph of 'imagined communities', Anderson acknowledged that his immediate prompt was the conflict between Vietnam, Pol Pot's Cambodia and China in 1978–79, 'the first *large scale conventional war*', he noted emphatically, 'waged by one revolutionary Marxist regime against another'. 'Since World War II,' he added, as though in debate with the Marxists, 'every successful revolution has defined itself in *national* terms.'

With an intellectual background in the borderlands between anthropology and political science, Anderson did not differ radically from other recent theorists in his comprehension of the nation as first and foremost an idea. Not for Anderson, however, the Marxist Eric Hobsbawm's certainty that that conception was a lie fostered by a self-interested social group. In Anderson's softer view, rather, the imagining occurred as much from below as from above, once the historic process of the invention of the first modern nations was set moving and speeded by the development of so-called 'print capitalism', the daily newspaper and the other agents of the dissemination of modern 'knowledge'.

The result of modernity was, therefore, a world of nations, a place of light and shadow, one where war was fought as eagerly for love of country as for hatred of the Other. 'Members of even the smallest nation will never know most of their fellow-members, meet them, or even hear of them,' Anderson conceded, 'yet in the minds of each lives the image of their communion.' As Anderson concluded: 'It is this fraternity that makes it possible, over the past two centuries, for so many millions of people, not so much to kill, as willingly to die for such limited imaginings.' After all, he added with what might be viewed now as a somewhat cloying optimism, reflecting the naively hopeful spirit of Jimmy Carter's USA: 'In an age when it is so common for progressive, cosmopolitan intellectuals (particularly in Europe?) to insist on the near-pathological character of nationalism, its roots in fear and hatred of the Other, and its affinities with racism, it is useful to remind ourselves that nations inspire love, and often profoundly self-sacrificing love.'

solved the riddle of permanent and ever-increasing prosperity while each nation is willing to forgo its independence for long enough to push through globalizing reforms, cut tariffs, eliminate the interference of unions in the free play of the market, and curb corrupt and inefficient sweetheart deals among the rapaciously rich and powerful. Yet this world policy, this universal ideology, does not deny the nation. Instead, capitalism regularly makes its assessment of its achievements and progress in national terms. Every week, *The Economist* publishes tables where national growth, inflation, production and stock-market level are recorded and compared. With the implied hierarchy and movement up and down such lists, the idea of a Darwinian struggle everywhere reappears, even while the globalizers dream of a universal happiness resulting from the virtuous application of their theory. The science of good economic management will have to coexist with the ambiguities of the nation, just as business ethics somehow make do with the distortions of advertising and profit-making.

The liberal polity is riven with another, more human, contradiction, as the journalist quoted above from *The Economist* unwittingly revealed. A misinterpreted past heroism, we were assured, is dangerous. Heroism needs a Hero, a Great Man (most often, but Great Women can easily be blended to the formula), a dominant individual. Since we live in a time of the constant evocation of such people, from political and commercial leaders to sports stars to celebrities whose only claim to significance is that they have somehow had fame ascribed to them, and we inhabit a lottery state where winners congratulate themselves daily after carrying off this or that prize and losers stay silent, Great People are harder and harder to escape. Yet their existence and presumed significance square uncertainly with the generalized 'community' embodied in the nation. If consistency is to be desired, then a National Hero can be one only if he or she combines heroism with self-abnegation. Rather, as the Marxist Antonio Gramsci envisaged an 'organic intellectual', resisting the Bolshevik delusion of being a vanguard, so, logically, a national hero should radiate from below and conceal and humbly deny any public leadership.

These and other stark inconsistencies are the explanation why, in the twenty-first century, nations are everywhere growing more anxious about who belongs and who does not, more ready to exclude the alien, more emphatic about the need for loyalty and only that. Liberal nations now launch preventive wars against enemies, painted in slapdash

Nations are everywhere growing more anxious about who belongs and who does not, more ready to exclude the alien, more emphatic about the need for loyalty and only that

manner as evil and 'mad' others. In the resulting battles, both military and civilian, the rule of law applies erratically. Habeas corpus, the need to prove guilt before summary execution, the scrupulous avoidance of civilian killing, all become trumpery matters at a time when the nation must urgently be protected from its foes. The globe, in other words, is made safe – but only for those who belong to virtuous nations. Those damned as the citizens of 'rogue states' (really rogue nations), the bad guys, have no future.

It is this equivocal present that provides the first spur to this account of the lights and shadows of nation-building since the Enlightenment. In that time of innocence, the emergence of nations and their happy and universal cohabitation seemed an easy process. Quickly, however, difficulties arose. How should one nation relate to the rest? How should nations in Europe, the continent that, through the nineteenth century, was the global centre of power and initiative, relate to the extra-European world? What if the people of a nation state were not all of the same language, culture and national purpose? What if the nation state was 'incomplete', since people of its language, culture and national purpose lived under another flag? What if immigrants transported other languages, cultures and ideals into a nationalized society? Should national unity be privileged over class and gender equality? How could the individual be both free and an integral part of a national community? Was national belonging a matter of education and imagination, 'all in the mind', or should it be defined by science of some kind, most malevolently by the pseudo-science of race? How should national idiosyncrasy relate to global class and gender issues, to global capitalism, to global peace and war? What happened when a locality in some eyes was a suppressed nation and in others' view was not?

The growth of nations has been repeatedly troubled by these and other dilemmas, and it is their history that will be tracked in this book. In each chapter, boxes display how historians and other social commentators have, over time, depicted the nation, its pomp and discontents. In its more orthodox narrative, starting with a review of the definitional complications of the nation, the book ponders the question whether proto-nations existed before the emergence of the terms 'nationality' and 'nationalism' at the end of the eighteenth century. Its major focus, however, is on the nineteenth and twentieth centuries and illuminates the achievements of nationalized peoples in these times as well as appraising the role of the nation in the terrible world wars of 1914–18 and 1939–45. The certainly failed and perhaps deluded hope of Marxism, Soviet-style, to favour internationalism, the state and class over nationalism, the market and ethnicity is assessed in Chapter 5. A final chapter investigates why the defeat of Nazi-fascist 'integral', aggressive and racial nationalism in 1945 and the dissolution of the USSR and its empire at the end of the 1980s have not yet brought universal peace and content-ment. In the new millennium, our belonging to nations still seems to vary between effects that are fair and foul. Our era of nations has not yet, it seems, resolved the scurfy history of humankind, and integral nationalism is very much back in business.

Notes

1 *The Economist*, 25 February 2006.

2 See B. Anderson, *Imagined Communities: Reflections on the Origin and Spread of Nationalism* (1983, London: Verso) for this term.

CHAPTER 1

Nationalism: strengths and contradictions, truths and lies

DULCE ET DECORUM EST, PRO PATRIA MORI (it is sweet and fitting to die for one's country). How often do we hear such sentiments expressed in today's world, at least metaphorically? When our sportspeople strive with all their might in this, that or the other game at the Olympics (where the number of sports spirals endlessly up), are they not selflessly giving themselves for the nation and its gold-medal tally? When our business-people tell us to buy their homemade products, are they not being virtuous? Setting aside their principled free-market individualism, do they not defend the collective because the nation's goods must also, by definition, be ours? When our politicians meet their fellows, can we not spot our representatives and, in the seemingly ever less secure world, feel better protected because, nestling on a lapel, will be a badge of our national flag? Is not the flag the holy symbol of what our soldiers died for in all the wars?

(There is typically no mention in this discourse of our killing in these battles. Nationalized war memorials have abandoned the earlier practice of celebrating emperors and generals instead to mourn 'our' deaths and suffering. They still ignore, however, the casualties we inflicted on others.) We rally around the fundamental symbols of our 'way of life' and, in so doing, we, the citizens of the nation, know that we possess sovereignty and identity. The national icons are what ensure that we are us. Our national values are the summit of morality.

The national icons are what ensure that we are us. Our national values are the summit of morality

The lie of the nation

Perhaps. *Dulce et decorum est pro patria mori*. The Latin saying has many resonances. It was coined by Horace, a poet–propagandist of the slave-based economy and conquering, multi-peopled empire of Rome under the canny Emperor Augustus. Yet the words were echoed in the twentieth century by a rather different poet, the Welshman Wilfred Owen. They form the most telling line of his bitter denunciation of trench warfare on the Western Front during the First World War. As the poem explains defiantly, these Latin words constitute the 'old lie' that drives men and even some women to pointless extinction, while, in Flanders, the imperial British army slogs it out with the imperial German army to the benefit of neither society. Of course, Owen uses the word *'patria'* (fatherland), rather than nation, perhaps importantly so, since it is not at all certain that imperial Britain and imperial Germany were 'nations', should that word be precisely defined. After all, was Lieutenant Owen British, or English, or Anglo-Saxon, or British imperial, or Welsh, or middle-class, or intellectual and male? As soon as the glitter of the nation is faced down, as soon as the music of the national song is stilled, as soon as the glory and sacrifice of the national military record and the devotion of national politicians to the safety of their people are questioned, defining the nation turns out to be the greatest conundrum in the history of human life since the French Revolution, if not before. In the twenty-first century, billions of people, if asked, are likely to assert that their identity is rooted primarily in their nation. Mysteriously, the liberal nation in modern times can embrace the individual and the family as well as the whole community. Modernity has been built 'on the twin pillars of the nuclear family which posed as an individual and the nation which posed as a nuclear family'.[1]

Paradoxes crowd in. As the French writer Ernest Renan remarked more than a century ago, the nation is nothing without falsehood. As we cheer our athletes, hail our business achievements, express our national family values, vote for our politicians, salute our flag, draw spiritual meaning from our countryside and claim eternity for ourselves, we distort history. We lie. Simultaneously, on our revolving globe and in the perpetually changing human condition, we tell a visceral truth.

Truth and falsehood intersect in their construction and continuously jostle each other in national and international practice

To rephrase Renan: no one can seriously plumb the history of nations and nationalism without realizing that truth and falsehood intersect in their construction and continuously jostle each other in national and international practice. The power of the national idea is steeled by the fact that, under its aegis, truth and falsehood, achievement and catastrophe, victory and victimhood, cannot easily be teased apart. In one perspective, nations since 1789 have flourished in a world characterized by scientific and material progress, social cohesion and popular contentment. While one industrial and technological revolution succeeded another, humans have become able to enjoy myriad options in their lives, unavailable to, and unimagined by, their ancestors. Yet, during that same period, nations have fostered exclusion, hierarchy, murder, genocide and local and world war. In the twenty-first century, stories of casual slaughter are an everyday event. Any account of a national chronicle and of the story of the nations must find room for success and failure, life and death, good and bad, the durable and the fickle.

Persuading contemporaries that the nation is as likely to be wrong as right remains a vexing task. Despite the problems that surface in any critical review of the era of nationalism, popular parlance, and presumably the popular mind that lies behind it, accepts the nation as self-evident and all-embracing. So carefully orthodox a work as the *Oxford English Dictionary* (OED) is confident that it can define 'nation'. Such a body, it says, is 'an extensive aggregate of persons, so closely associated with each other by common descent, language or history as to form a distinct race or people, usually organized as a separate political state and occupying a definite territory'. The OED's first example of the usage in English is then taken from a source dating to 1300, that is, to the reign of King Edward I, the French-speaking English ruler who viciously suppressed the Scots and the Welsh. The second reference is drawn from John Wyclif, prototype

English Protestant, around 1380, that is, during the reign of King Richard II; the Lollard preacher hailed the 'gospels of Crist written in Englische to moost lernyng of our nacion'. John of Gaunt, Richard's uncle, has had placed into his mouth by William Shakespeare, writing two centuries later, the classic speech about the island kingdom as a natural jewel, impregnable against the perpetual attacks of others, a sacred soil rendered fertile through many generations by a people's blood:

This royal throne of kings, this sceptred isle,
This earth of majesty, this seat of Mars,
This other Eden, demi-paradise,
This fortress built by nature for herself
Against infection and the hand of war,
This happy breed of men, this little world,
This precious stone set in the silver sea,
Which serves it in the office of a wall
Or as a moat defensive to a house
Against the envy of less happier lands.

In ordinary discourse, the nation seems as natural and as permanent as the air we breathe.

The lie of the land

Much begins with geography. But the world is not uniform; it is, rather, sundered by oceans, seas, rivers and mountain chains. Each seems eternal, and therefore 'god-given' if a deity is needed to comprehend or justify existence. How simple, then, to conclude that nations are a geopolitical datum. John of Gaunt's England is what it is because the sea beats on its coasts and severs it from those inferior realms where the skittish French and other envious foreigners live. Japan's long history is set apart by its natural separation from the Chinese mainland. Once its new settlers moved over the Alleghenies, the USA had a manifest destiny to rule the American continent from sea to shining sea. The Ethiopian mountains, deserts and the Nile mark out another empire, just as the endless steppes of Central Asia justify Russian rule from the Baltic to the Pacific. The Pyrenees cut off France from Spain, while the flow of the Danube and Rhine rivers maps the borders of Germandom. For the Greek writer Nikos Kazantzakis, it was light that decided all: 'The factor which renders Greece's mountains, villages and soil buoyant and immaterial is the light. In Italy, the light is soft and feminine, in Ionia extremely gentle and full of oriental yearning, in Egypt thick and voluptuous. In Greece the light is entirely spiritual.'[2] As such high-flown phrases indicate, each nationalism owes something to European romanticism with its new alertness at the end of the eighteenth century to the alleged beauty and meaningfulness of nature. To each nation thereafter, geography seemed to decree a god-given place, a god-given soil.

Yet, a moment's thought repudiates any neat explanation of history based on geographical determinism. The British Isles contain Scots, Welsh, Irish, Cornish and, over the centuries, myriad immigrants (including the Anglo-Saxon conquerors of Roman Britain), with histories transported into England from abroad. John of Gaunt's sacred soil is now familiarly trod by West Indian, Pakistani, Polish and Iranian Britons. Koreans and *Burakumin* are part of the Japanese population mix. Portuguese, Catalans, Basques, North African immigrants and not only the Spanish live south of the Pyrenees. Mountain watersheds rarely mark out borders that coincide fully with language or culture. Germans live south of the Alps. 'Italian' Trieste lies east of the Balkan-style Carso. If a plain or the direction of a river flow fosters a natural expansion, then how is it that only some of those who live in its environs have spread their state borders? As soon as geography is read in detail, rather than in some broad sweep, the naturalness of national space vanishes and the horror of ethnic cleansing, designed to make people and land coincide, emerges.

As soon as geography is read in detail, the naturalness of national space vanishes and the horror of ethnic cleansing, designed to make people and land coincide, emerges

The most sinister manifestation of geographical determinism was a key part of the race theory that debouched into Nazism. For modern racists, mostly nationalists seeking a 'logical' conclusion to their theorizing, the fundamental assumption was that the fate of humankind was decided by 'blood and soil'. In this view, which malignly mixed a (pseudo-) science of blood-stocks with a spiritual and religious evocation of nature, a territory was sacred to its nation or race, the roots of which deeply penetrated a native land. The human condition was as organic as the flourishing of a particular flora or fauna.

Nazism was defeated and destroyed in 1945; its special history in regard to nationalism is discussed in a later chapter. Yet, the death of Adolf Hitler did not signal the erasing of concepts of blood and soil (or race). Over the past decades, those ideas have come flooding back into acceptable discourse and are once more a part of national identity. Why else, after all, did the peripatetic and populist Pope John Paul II, heir to the oldest international organization on earth but steeped in the thought patterns of Polish nationalism, over and over again kiss the soil (in practice, usually the airport tarmac) of the numerous countries he visited? As he knelt, he was preaching that the universal Christian church, for all its global commitment and Romanizing habits, yearned to commune with each nation of the globe. His religion was sacred. But so, too, was their soil.

Part of the paraphernalia of nationalism had long been an anthropomorphic naturalizing of birds, animals and vegetation as carrying human meaning – the Nazis nourished a 'green' side – and such habits have become entrenched in recent times. The kangaroo stands for Australia, the eagle for the USA, the bear for Russia, the monkey for China. The humming bird has fluttered nationhood on to the flag of Papua New Guinea since that country gained independence in 1975. In the first world, anxious environmentalists campaign for the elimination from national soil of 'alien' plants and trees. In Western Australia, migrant sparrows are shot on sight and purists wonder whether the kookaburra, 'native' to eastern Australia but not the west, should be expelled from local trees. Throughout Australia, campaigners remonstrate against the human affection for the domestic cat, cruel, foreign and 'European' (despite the feline's apparent emergence in ancient Egypt), slayer of local fauna. Householders uproot roses and deciduous trees, finding solace only when their back gardens are stocked with 'bush plants' (however adapted in the nursery to suburban life). Yet the migration of flora and fauna is an age-old process and one that, across the millennia, has allowed and allows humankind to eat. Only some sort of environmentalist Adolf Hitler should seriously want to extirpate the eucalyptus trees of Ethiopia or Italy, the shiraz vines that have spread beyond Persia, the sheep that fatten on grasses in many places (and the rats that flourish everywhere). All are migrants; none is as it was.

In the European Union and the USA, the massive subsidies that are directed at agriculture and the nostalgic rhetoric about how an authentic camembert or Cumberland sausage or ground-beef hamburger should 'really' taste similarly endorse the idea that we are made by our soil. In Britain, fans of fox hunting, who are themselves, in the main, city men and women, claim loudly that a ban on it will destroy the national character mystically reinforced when 'the unspeakable' can freely pursue 'the inedible'. Even though urbanization is one of the most evident processes in every society over the past two centuries, the romantic view that reality is found in the countryside (no matter how altered by human habitation and the practice of farming) is treasured by many city dwellers whose actual visits to the land are rare and fleeting.

The discourse about 'first peoples' is full of parallel argument that the aboriginal inhabitants of a particular territory (its particularity being by definition of recent design) deserve redress from their present repressors because the real natives of a particular territory have lived unchanged and in blessedly intimate understanding of 'their' soil for so long. In contemporary Australia, land rights are offered on the understanding that the connection of Aborigines to the soil has been continuous and coherent over many centuries, an occupation that is meant to make such people the holy vehicles of a special national spirituality. Only the land, it seems, can measure time in a genuine way, rather as an ancient tree recalls each season with a ring in its trunk. It is the alleged special continuity of nature that renders our nation better and nobler than that of others and, with some degree of contradiction, expresses our eternity. Middle-class Australians like to preen themselves that a properly worshipful treatment of 'Aboriginal history' and so a connection of all Australians with the soil will accord the whole nation '60 000 years' of history, a tally that will overwhelm any absurd and patronizing 'European' (a word that in the Australian context often means British) assertion that ours is a callowly new country, born with white settlement in 1788, or with constitutional framing in 1901, or with the opting for a (partially) independent foreign policy after the fall of Singapore in 1941.

Forked tongues

In the new millennium, enthusiasm for the national soil can be found everywhere. An open endorsement of the concept of national bloodstocks is a less

In the new millennium, enthusiasm for the national soil can be found everywhere

universally appealing line since it may smack of Nazi-style racism. What usually happens in this argument is that the idea of god-given geography is diluted into the looser belief that the nation is constituted by its language, culture and history. Linguistic maps show where nations were or ought to be. People, it is assumed, know that they belong to their nation because they speak one language, while foreigners use other tongues. When post-1945 Australia was convincing itself that it could cope with non-British migrants, a social scientist announced that no good Australian wanted newcomers to use their 'language' – his assumption apparently was that foreigners just spoke foreign – in 'public places'. The French Academy zealously, if ineffectually, strives to expunge franglais from demeaning the glorious and ancient national language. The framers of the OED boasted that their sensible Englishness was reflected in their readiness to admit linguistic change (but only at the borders of the vast empire of words their dictionary hammered into place). All modern European nation states were justified linguistically. Italians, it was argued, spoke Italian and so were Italian; Norwegians spoke Norwegian and so must leave the Swedish crown; Latvians spoke Latvian and should not be gobbled up by a Russian or Soviet empire. Moreover, when identity politics stimulated the idea that migration made it possible to hold double nationality and be a German American or a Jamaican Englishman or a Muslim Frenchwoman, then the 'minority' culture was usually most easily tolerated as a variety of music, a dress, a cuisine or a second language.

Yet, once again, any assumption that the national linguistic story is clear-cut is false. We may love and treasure our native tongue and its literature but, in reality, language is another fragile base from which to master time. Nicholas Ostler, in his universal history of the word, has asserted that there are some 6800 languages still existing on the planet. Yet, he adds, the 12 most frequently spoken languages account for more than half the global population. Ostler complains that one tongue dies out every fortnight (although his own text is riddled with nationalist-seeming assumptions that human difference is automatically expressed in language groups that compete one with another in a sort of linguistic Darwinian struggle of the fittest or luckiest). Even if autonomous zones are generously assumed to be proto-nations, then the present world possesses only some

200 states, and the inhabitants of many of these speak such great imperial languages as English, Spanish, Mandarin Chinese and a variant of Arabic. Language cannot assure that you are Canadian or Paraguayan or Yemeni and, as Ostler argues, 'most of the people in the world are still bilingual'.[3] But, plainly, arithmetic demonstrates that the possession of a distinct language does not equate with membership in a state. Moreover, languages, like nature, are perpetually affected by human manipulation. Modern Hebrew, Greek, Italian – each is a way of speech that was invented after the nations of Israel, Greece and Italy came into existence or where the linguistic invention was part of the political process of nation-building. When Italy commenced its life as some form of nation state in 1860–61, the largest single language group in the country was that 2.5 per cent or so of the population who spoke Latin, the antique speech of the Catholic Church. So-called dialect – that is, a language that, for some political reason, has not been called a language – long remained the favoured tongue for the majority of inhabitants of the Italian peninsula and for those who scattered from it around the world in emigration. The imposition of the national language on Italians had to await the cultural adaptation brought by the spread of national television-viewing in the 1960s and 1970s.

Nor are other languages different in their trajectories. One language is being perpetually buffeted by another, and, as a result, borrowing always takes place. Since the beginning of time, human beings have migrated, and every city has been a polyglot place. In the first century AD, the Roman writer Seneca (born in Cordoba) already knew that, in every urban agglomeration 'a large proportion of the population is immigrant'.[4] With the spread of urbanization and the ever accelerating global migration, we all live surrounded by multiple tongues. Moreover, since 'civilization' and the city are in many ways the products of each other, cultures reach their summit only where comprehension comes in varied phrasing. As the Italo-German, part Jewish, perhaps part Slovene, or maybe Magyar writer 'Italo Svevo' (real name Ettore Schmitz), some time citizen of the Habsburg Empire, some time of Fascist Italy, put it optimistically, it is 'the fate of humankind to live in mixed tenses'.[5]

Certainly, washed by a restless sea of linguistic change, none speaks as once their 'ancestors' did. We make our languages at least as much as our languages make us. Different classes pronounce their words in different ways (a matter that has long been the mainstay of the humour of Britain and many other societies). So, too, urban dwellers and people from the countryside phrase themselves differently. For millennia, yokels have been derided as yokels because they cannot, or do not want to, master the phrasing and intonation of the town. In old age, as death approaches, speech changes, just as it more obviously does when we are very young, when we are teenagers or when we make love. Vocabularies and speech patterns can be gendered. It may be true that the first plank of much nation-building was an education policy designed to render a population literate, to do so in a homogeneous national language possessed of precise grammatical rules and so, to repeat the memorable title of a study of the process in France after 1870, to forge 'peasants into Frenchmen'.[6] Yet, despite states' attempts to channel words in their cause and their cause alone, languages have gone on living and changing, preserving a life of their own outside government control. Perhaps the most notorious example of controlled speech was the special vocabulary and thought patterns that the totalitarianism of the Soviets yearned to impose on the populace of all the Russias. Some new Soviet men and women did adopt identities dependent on this new language. The vast majority of the peoples of the Soviet empire, however, heard and sullenly disobeyed, opting either to be 'Nicodemic', that is, consciously hypocritical when they had to spout party words, or otherwise finding means to go on speaking to themselves in their own way. As a historian, born and resident in Australia, I am more at home speaking to other historians of whatever nationality (these days with the speech often being the typed phrases of email) than in talking with Australian farmers or sportspeople. When I do have discourse with such people, I self-consciously switch my phrasing, vocabulary (and attitudes) so as not to reveal too blatantly how alien I, or part of me, is in my 'homeland'.

Cultures are at least as mutable and varied as are languages and are similarly affected by factors other than that of national difference. One of the more passionate and bizarre games of the modern world is the competition to be old. In Fascist Italy, Mussolini boasted of Italy's '3000 years of history' and his Fascist dictatorship made the (alleged) birthday of Rome into a national holiday. Imperial Japan was sure that the *kokutai* – the national polity – had proceeded unchanged also for 3000 years, and its longevity did not only match the Italians but also demonstrated to all the supreme virtue of the Japanese nation and 'race'. In democratic Japan, even today, conservatives fear that admitting a female succession to the Chrysanthemum

Cultures are at least as mutable and varied as are languages and are similarly affected by factors other than that of national difference

Throne will shatter the *kokutai*. The English and French frequently bespoke their own effortless superiority over newer and so more juvenile peoples by maintaining that they had become nation states in the early Middle Ages, if not before. Zionists in modern-day Israel argue that they have restored the Jewish state that flourished before Christ and the Roman overthrow of the Temple. Ethiopians justify their lingering African empire by claiming the Queen of Sheba as an antecedent.

Food is similarly likely to be highlighted on a list of national distinction. Their fondness for spaghetti makes Italians Italian. The Irish drink in their nation with a glass of Guinness. The English have long replenished their red blood with (over-cooked) roast beef. Chopsticks and rice are naturally Chinese. Aboriginal peoples conserve secret and spiritual knowledge of native foods.

But again, when subject to analysis, our feeding is soon revealed to be another complex and changing matter. After all, the flesh of animals and plants, affected by modern technology well before present worries about genetic modification, is not the same in taste or texture as it was centuries ago. Prepared food is little different. One historian with a yen for irony has demonstrated that 'Calabrian cuisine' was invented during nineteenth-century migration to the USA.[7] Much 'ethnic food', cherished at moments of multicultural display, has little to do with its actual consumption in places of origin, whether at the time of departure of a particular migrant group or now. The foamy coffee consumed in innumerable cappuccino strips in cities around the world, with the variants of skinnycino (with low-fat milk), babycino (froth only, marketed to the very young) and 'cups of chino' (for those with a weak knowledge of Italian and an inventive cast in linguistic adaptation), can scarcely be assumed to be the drink first consumed by eighteenth-century Parisians. In the age of celebrity television cooks, even 'English food' cannot be relied on to consist of cholesterol-laden slabs of blackened roast or fried meat, bolstered by chips or vegetables done to death by overboiling.

Rags on dungheaps

Food may be the most practical symbol of national identity, but it retains a humdrum character that does not automatically invoke the sacred in the way that some other alleged aspects of the nation do. In this regard, the most celebrated icons are neither the tax collector nor the recruiting sergeant but, rather, the flag and the national anthem. In every society, coloured pennons had been an accustomed part of celebration in the premodern world. The first modern flag, however, was the tricolour of Revolutionary France, a society anxious to justify or cloak its radicalism by deploying helpful histories and eager to replace the ceremony of its Bourbon predecessors with a sacrality of its own. Since 1789, the citizens of every nation have felt obliged to rally around a flag, and a discourse has grown inscribing the meaning of the nation, its past, present and future, on to coloured cloth. Benito Mussolini, in his socialist youth, may have been sardonic about the green, white and red flag of Italy, dismissing it as 'a rag on a dungheap'. Entrepreneurs may have deployed the flag on parts of the body that are not evidently sublime: Union flag panties can be purchased with the knowing slogan 'Mind the gap'. But, among the more conservative politicians and the spokespeople of returned soldiers, a discourse has grown that regards the flag as so holy an item that any criticism of it amounts to blasphemy. In the contemporary USA, flag-burning is frequently damned as a sad carryover from the social decay of anti-Vietnam days, and discussion continues over whether any misuse of the flag should automatically lead to a long stretch in jail. Soldiers in real battles and sportspeople in fake ones utilize the flag as the symbol of their unity and purpose. When they are spiritually wrapped in the flag, engendering a modern mystery of transubstantiation, its threads become the nation.

En-chant-ed by the nation

Even more obvious in its holy purpose is the so-called 'national anthem', the latter word underlining the carryover from past universal religions and the verses sung in church to the festivals of the nation. The anthem, too, is a modern invention. 'God Save the King [Queen]' is credited to composition by Henry Carey in 1740. It had, however, been adapted from a French tune, used under Louis XIV, written by the maybe French, maybe Italian (he was born in Florence), Giam Battista Lulli. Its anodyne first verse is usually the only one sung, but a version of the second verse runs more aggressively:

O Lord our God arise,
Scatter her enemies
And make them fall;
Confound their politics,
Frustrate their knavish tricks,
On Thee our hopes we fix,
God save us all!

In any case, the chief model for the national anthem was once again France, where the *Marseillaise* was composed in 1792 as a militant battle hymn of the republican forces (as its first two verses make plain):

Allons enfants de la Patrie
Le jour de gloire est arrivé!
Contre nous de la tyrannie
L'étendard sanglant est levé
Entendez-vous dans nos campagnes
Mugir ces féroces soldats?
Ils viennent jusque dans vos bras.
Égorger vos fils, vos compagnes!

Aux armes citoyens!
Formez vos bataillons!
Marchons, marchons!
Qu'un sang impur
Abreuve nos sillons!

Que veut cette horde d'esclaves
De traîtres, de rois conjurés?
Pour qui ces ignobles entraves
Ces fers des longtemps préparés?
Français, pour nous, ah! Quel outrage
Quels transports il doit exciter!
C'est nous qu'on ose méditer
De rendre à l'antique esclavage!

It is true that, on occasion, there have been complications in the history of national songs. Fascist Italy, for example, could never make up its mind whether the party anthem *Giovinezza* or the

'Royal March' (*Marcia reale*) should be played on official occasions. Usually the compromise was that both tunes had to resound, a habit that made for long ceremonies. Nor did national musical ambiguity cease in Italy after 1945. After the fall of the dictatorship and the establishment of a republic, the Italians took as their anthem the so-called 'Mameli Hymn', *Fratelli d'Italia*, a patriotic song of the nineteenth-century Risorgimento, which is dated and sexist in its evocation of Italian brothers but not sisters. Australia, turning its back on the British, or European, or imperial God save the Queen decided, in the 1970s, to hold a referendum among its people to select a successor, offering four choices. Victory went to the most worthy or meaningless 'Advance Australia Fair', an anthem that, with verbal desperation, feels obliged to remind Australians that they are 'girt by sea'.

With that sad irony that abounds in its history, the USSR, about whose tortured engagement with nationalism more can be found below, adopted as its special song the *Internationale*, allegedly composed by a socialist worker after the brutal suppression of the Paris Commune in 1871, and thereafter spreading from French into all languages. Rather than hymning a nation, this anthem hailed the global struggle of working men and women. Moreover, the *Internationale*, like the *Marseillaise*, has lengthy and complex lyrics and is, therefore, based on a highly optimistic view of the desire among the masses to learn and understand. More recent anthems are shorter and simpler and can sometimes be remembered by sportspeople as, clenched right fists on hearts, they sing them before a match or after a victory, and by the crowds who watch them and join in the patriotic fervour unleashed by alcohol, fun and the resounding of the holy music of the nation.

History yoked

Geography, language, songs and symbols are all very well, but, among the fundamental qualities that members of a nation are meant to share, the most commonly evoked is history, meaning not so much the professional and critical discipline of that name as the past or rather the seamless connection between past, present and future. In the popular rendering of the national story, the usual way of reading the path across time is a Whig one – an account that emphasizes progress and gain. Nations start small and grow bigger. Their economies prosper from one decade to the next. Their peoples suffer on occasion but work, triumph and grow happy. Did not Titus Livy, the

Nations start small and grow bigger. Their economies prosper from one decade to the next. Their peoples suffer on occasion but work, triumph and grow happy

great historian of the classical Roman republic, argue at the start of his lengthy work 'If any nation deserves the privilege of claiming a divine ancestry, that nation is our own'?[8] Later, did he not write off the military achievements of Alexander the Great as extensive merely because he had thrust south and east and so avoided having to do battle with his Roman contemporaries?[9] Is not the final proof of a nation its existence in history and the concurrent demonstration that eternity is its reality or due?

Once again, however, a problem arises. Its essence is the uneasy relationship between the scientific pretensions of academic history-writing once it spread into universities a century and a half ago, its 'noble dream' of objectivity, empathy and truth, and the more adaptable, not to say shamelessly false, harnessing of the past to the national cause in 'memory' and in popular history. Yet academic history is another arena much subject to national will. It is a commonplace that the discipline of history has been yoked into chronological lockstep with that of the nation. Still in the new millennium, probably the majority of published pieces of historical research and of courses taught in universities throughout the globe have the nation as their basis. Back in the Middle Ages, Geoffrey of Monmouth, Bishop of St Asaph 1151–55, set an example of a kind. His *Historia Regum Britannie* managed to invent a past for the 'kingdom of Britain' that could be pursued into the mists of time and included numerous moments of glory when British monarchs victoriously acceded to the throne of the Roman Empire. None of the events he described so fulsomely actually happened.

In the nineteenth century, matters were not so different. Jules Michelet in France and George Bancroft in the USA crafted sonorous prose to laud the national story of their states. In newer nations, the same vocabulary and attitudes could appear even in our own times. In Australia, during the 1970s C.M.H. ('Manning') Clark, with heavy debt to biblical phrasing, became the most public forger of an antipodean 'new nationalism'. Back in the nineteenth century, there could be other contradictions. The Czech nation found its chronicler in Frantisek Palacky (1798–1876), an author whose multi-volume national history was composed in German and only later translated into Czech. Similarly, every Balkan people had the cause of the nation explicated and justified by written history, with the Greeks, who 'reacquired' a state of a kind in the 1820s and at once depicted themselves as the natural heirs of Pericles and Demosthenes, providing the lead. As history professionalized, austere depositories of research such as the *American Historical Review* (founded 1895), the *English Historical Review* (1886) and *Rivista Storica Italiana* (1884) concentrated most on American, British and Italian history, while *Revue Historique* (1876) and *Historische Zeitschrift* (1859) did the same for the French and German pasts. International breakdown and its resultant military conflict were likely to prompt historians to locate past justification for their nation, with the so-called 'Great War' of 1914–18 being a towering example. Then almost every historian endorsed, and indeed enthused over, warfare, with an Italian nationalist taking matters to the logical extreme when he talked confidently of how truth itself must obey the law of nations. Italian truth, he said, was simply not the same as German or French or Russian truth.

Led by the great German Leopold von Ranke (1795–1886), with his emphasis on the discipline's need for philological accuracy, academic historians may have proclaimed that they served a scientific and rational discipline designed to pave the path of humankind towards perfection but, in practice at least, most writers until 1919 couched their learned works in national terms, recounted a national past and offered tempting glimpses of a better national future. As a recent commentator has noted: 'Modern history was born in the nineteenth century, conceived and developed as an instrument of European nationalism.'[10] A century later, most professional historians, reacting against the infection of nationalism at history's birth, are alert to over-writing the nation. Quite a few accept the position best put by the Marxist Eric Hobsbawm that no 'serious historians of nations and nationalism can be a committed political nationalist'. 'Nationalism', Hobsbawm stated sternly, 'requires too much belief in what is patently not so.'[11]

Eric Hobsbawm

The most coherent critic of nationalism among the past generation of analysts of the subject is the great Marxist historian Eric Hobsbawm. His two key books are (edited with Terence Ranger) *The Invention of Tradition* (1983, Cambridge: Cambridge University Press) and *Nations and Nationalism Since 1980: Programme, Myth, Reality* (1990, Cambridge: Cambridge University Press).

Born in June 1917 in Alexandria in Egypt, then under quasi-imperial British guidance, Hobsbawm grew into a mixed heritage. His mother was the daughter of a Viennese jeweller; his father an English-born Jew, deluding himself that he could become upwardly mobile through adroit business dealing. Carrying in his mind some imprint from the fading multinational Habsburg empire, the still buoyant multinational British empire and a Jewishness that might prove cosmopolitan, 'European' or Zionist, Hobsbawm passed his childhood for a while in Vienna and for a while in Berlin. He endured the early and despairing deaths of his parents, destroyed by the Depression and so by business and its failures. In response, he joined the Young Communist League 'to serve the world revolution', watched from a school bench while Hitler was jockeyed into power by old German nationalist elites and escaped a threatening fate since, courtesy of his father, he could call himself a British subject. After moving to London in April 1933, Hobsbawm proceded through Cambridge to a distinguished British academic career, if neither in his work nor in his most intimate beliefs did he abandon the cosmopolitan Marxist hope that 'the number of our Members be unlimited'. In diagnosing the nation as the canker of the modern political order, Hobsbawm remained a Marxist, while simultaneously reflecting the dilemma of many people of Jewish background in a world of nations where opting to be a 'non-Jewish Jew' was becoming more taxing.

For Hobsbawm, nations have a distinct, a truncated and an invented history. Searching, as a Marxist should, for scientific 'truth', Hobsbawm contended that the lie was what predominated in the national story. 'Nations', he wrote, 'do not make states and nationalisms but the other way round.' There was nothing organic about them. They did not spring inexorably and eternally from blood and soil. Rather, they were the product intellectually of 'the lesser examination passing classes', a group who battened on to the processes allowing for, and resulting from, the spread of the modern state. Greedy for fame and pleasure, they were ready to risk the health of the people of the globe for their own petty advancement, most readily occurring in their own petty invented nations. Such downmarket purveyors of culture were the classic 'inventors of tradition', often unscientific historians or other cynical and importunate vendors of the past, who contorted history for the benefit of the present. Ruthlessly, they combed the past for (im)moral tales that could seem to prove the eternal virtue of their nation and justify the damning of those enemies who, by definition, had always sought to overthrow and destroy the primary group. Hobsbawm wanted to be a citizen of the world and not of some restricted part of it, a Zionist nation state called Israel after 1948 being in his view an especially flawed construction. Even 'fundamentalism', Hobsbawm eventually wrote in the still innocent 1990, drew strength from claims for '*universal* truth'. Nationalism, he pronounced, by contrast malignly and 'by definition excludes from its purview all who do not belong to its own "nation", i.e. the vast majority of the human race.'

Yet Hobsbawm's internationalist Marxism was scarcely the winning ideology of the late twentieth century and early twenty-first century. Moreover, his austere critique of nationalism was made at a time when the role of history as the training ground of administrators and executives was already being lost to economics and law, and when universities were facing increasing difficulties in justifying too lavish state (and so national) funding for this, as for other, 'useless' humanities. It was true that the human predilection for seeking and finding lessons from the past had not disappeared. But, in the present framing of usable pasts, what has often happened is that professional historians have been ousted by popular ones, more cheerful about manipulating the national story to present advantage. The past may still circle around us and lighten our gloom, but it is less likely to be a critical past (at least in regard to the nation) than it might have been a generation ago. As the twenty-first century unfolds, we are again hearing that the past that matters is 'ours', and so above all that of our nation. Some historians, and certainly the author of this book, may locate shadows as well as lights in every national past, but the urge to cleanse history of its ambiguities seems in our present world to be a process hard to resist, one that threatens to sweep too academically critical analyses into irrelevance. In the twenty-first century, each nation is not ashamed to demand its own integral history and, by its possession, seeks to impose its own final solution on to the actual contradictions of humankind's fretted and fretful past (and future).

Notes

1 Y. Slezkine, *The Jewish century* (2004, Princeton, NJ: Princeton University Press), p. 44.

2 N. Kazantzakis, *Report to Greece* (1973, London: Faber & Faber), p. 164.

3 N. Ostler, *Empires of the Word: A Language History of the World* (2005, London: Harper Collins), pp. 7, 543.

4 L.A. Seneca, *Dialogues and letters* (ed. C.D.N. Costa) (1997, Harmondsworth: Penguin), p. 8.

5 P.N. Furbank, *Italo Svevo: The Man and the Writer* (1966, London: Secker and Warburg), p. 204.

6 E. Weber, *Peasants into Frenchmen: The Modernization of Rural France* (1976, Stanford, CA: Stanford University Press).

7 P. Ortoleva, 'Tradition and abundance: reflections on Italian-American foodways', *Altreitalie*, 1992, 7, p. 56.

8 T. Livy, *The Early History of Rome* (ed. A. De Sélincourt) (1960, Harmondsworth: Penguin), p. 17.

9 T. Livy, *Rome and Italy* (ed. B. Radice) (1982, Harmondsworth: Penguin), pp. 239–41.

10 P. Geary, *The Myth of Nations: The Medieval Origins of Europe* (2002, Princeton, NJ: Princeton University Press), p. 15.

11 E. Hobsbawm, *Nations and Nationalism since 1780: Programme, Myth, Reality* (1980, Cambridge: Cambridge University Press), p. 12.

CHAPTER 2

Nationalism before nations; nations before nationalism

BELONGING TO A NATION, it has been established, gives men and women comfort through the illusion of their resultant eternity. But the great majority of the discourse on nations and nationalism has come into existence only over the past two centuries. How, then, when they lacked this vocabulary, did human beings before the Enlightenment conceive of their identity? Is it possible to locate nationalism before nation states came into existence, or nations before nationalism?

The eternal nation?

One commentator with sardonic thoughts on the matter was the Dutch humanist Desiderius Erasmus, for a time resident in England and writing in Latin:

Now, . . . Nature had implanted . . . a sort of communal variety in every nation and city. Consequently the British think they have a monopoly, amongst other things, of good looks, musical talent and fine food. The Scots pride themselves on their nobility and the distinction of their royal connexions as much as on their subtlety in dialectic. The French lay claim to polite manners, the Parisians demand special recognition for their theological acumen which they think exceeds nearly everyone else's. The Italians usurp culture and eloquence, and hence they are all happy congratulating themselves on being the only civilized race of men. In this kind of happiness the Romans take first place, still blissfully dreaming of the past glories of Rome, while the Venetians have their own opinion of their noble descent to keep them happy. Meanwhile the Greeks, as the originators of the arts, imagine they should still share the honours of the illustrious heroes of their past; while the Turks and all the real barbarian riff-raff actually demand recognition for their religion and pour scorn on Christians for their superstition. The Jews go even further, still faithfully awaiting their Messiah and clinging fast to their Moses to this very day. The Spaniards admit no rival in the glories of war, while the Germans boast of their height and their knowledge of the magic arts.[1]

This text might seem decisive testimony that, in one of the most acute and wide-ranging minds of the era, it was assumed that nationality existed and had long existed. It might simultaneously seem demonstrated that those social scientists who want to claim a primordial or near-primordial ethnic sense and who are certain that the nations were implanted into people's minds well before the creation of the nation state are correct. Here might seem to be the proof that national differences amount to a 'deposit' left by 'collective experience'.[2]

England for ever

Theorists are not alone in holding such views. Present-day medieval history writing is, for example, full of confident assertions of longstanding national identity. The biographer of the English warrior–king Henry V (1413–22) claims that he was brilliantly able to deploy his charisma to 'stir up national sentiment in favour of himself and his cause'.[3] A monkish chronicle of his reign, the *Gesta Henrici Quinti*, maintained that the king had been applauded in his deeds by 'the English nation', who were themselves 'God's people'. The chronicler was thereby echoing the language that he had found in the Bible and the phrasing there about the 'nations' flowed, with whatever altered meaning, eventually into the vocabulary of nationalism.

In his glories, medievalist historians continue, Henry V was a great contrast with Richard II (1377–99), a monarch who 'divided the nation and paid the price' of deposition, being overthrown by a 'national uprising'.[4] Even earlier kings are eagerly nationalized. Richard I (1189–99), who notoriously spent hardly any time in England, preferring to war in the Holy Land and France, is said by his biographer to have represented 'the English nation, a man whose wars were demonstrations of English superiority over other nations especially the French'.[5]

Another scholar, who located the 'first English empire' as existing between 1093 and 1343, did admit this realm's eventual disintegration but, in his view, even before 1066, Anglo-Saxon England was becoming 'a powerfully imagined society, a nation-state' and was already evincing an English primacy in nationhood. 'In past-oriented and past-validating societies,' it was explained (but which societies are not?), 'control and exploitation of the past are critical to credibility in the present . . . The very early institutional maturity and self-definition of the English state and the tight weave of its power structures, ethnic self-profile, and historical mythology gave it remarkable resilience and cohesion. England,' it was asserted patriotically, was 'much the earliest and the most enduring of European nation states.'[6]

Geoffrey of Monmouth

According to the plainly nationalist editor of its current Penguin paperback edition (1966), the *Historia Regum Britannie* (the History of the Kings of Britain), completed around 1136 in the early days of the (disastrous) reign of the Norman-English King Stephen, bears the 'same relationship' to the story of 'early British inhabitants' of the UK 'as do the seventeen historical books of the Old Testament, from Genesis to Esther, to the early history of the Israelites in Palestine'.

The author of what is therefore implied to be the bible of the British nation was a monk known as Geoffrey of Monmouth. He is thought to have died in 1155 as Bishop of St Asaph in north-east Wales, although it is likely he never visited his bishopric. As a medieval scholar has put it in somewhat unreconstructed phrasing, probably 'Geoffrey was a normanised Celt, perhaps of Breton descent, although we cannot be sure of his exact racial extraction.' Geoffrey did his writing while living in Oxford after 1129 as a secular canon of the college of St George, dissolved 1149.

The *History* purports to cover the story of Britain, 'the best of islands', the happy place that 'provides in unfailing plenty everything that is suited to the use of human beings', from the misty past to the fifth-century arrival of the Saxons. Britain's eponymous first king, named Brutus, was the great-grandson of Aeneas (Geoffrey had been reading Virgil and Homer). Brutus, after committing parricide by destined accident, was expelled from Italy to Greece. There he met up with other Trojan refugees, whom he eventually led to the occupation of the island of Albion. He founded London and called it 'New Troy'.

Thereafter, Geoffrey's story moves on from one glorious victory to the next. After Roman occupation, British kings regularly invade the continent and assume imperial powers. The last half of the book is devoted to the derring-do of 'King Arthur', the last British hero. In these marvellous times, Geoffrey reports, 'Britain had reached such a standard of sophistication that it excelled all other kingdoms in its general affluence, the richness of its decorations, and the courteous behaviour of its inhabitants' – Camelot indeed.

The work was of course written in Latin, the universal language of the Church that Geoffrey served and, although there was soon a translation into the Welsh vernacular, the *History*'s greater early influence was in Brittany and what was coming to be called France. There, Chrétien de Troyes and other poets used Geoffrey as a source book for courtly romance. More scrupulous monkish chroniclers were not slow to recognize the fabulous nature of the great part of Geoffrey's history and dismissed his work acerbically. Although the Penguin editor claims that 'history keeps peeping through the fiction', Geoffrey's work is best read as a piece of literature, with its main historical value the insight it can offer into the political and religious subtleties of the twelfth-century Anglo-French world. Yet, for students of the nation and nationalism, the *History of the Kings of Britain* is significant as a shameless but amusing early medieval precursor of the invention of historical pasts that was to become so common in the nineteenth century and is still to be found in the more popular histories of contemporary nation states.

Eternal France

The French are not behindhand in voicing similar claims to national primacy. The great *Annales* historian Fernand Braudel won fame as the theorist of a triple-decked historical chronology.

According to his analysis, the short-term events of politics mattered less than did the slow-moving, deep currents of the *longue durée*. Braudel's most celebrated work traced the history of the entire littoral of the Mediterranean 'in the age of Philip II' but, actually, over a rather longer time period. To some extent, Braudel always wrote as a historian from the south of France, looking out to the Inland Sea. Yet he was very much the patriotic Frenchman, giving weight to the *longue durée* in order to paper over the mere events of the 'strange defeat', social disunity and political dishonour of France's Second World War.[7]

When he contemplated his nation's story, Braudel was proud to walk in the footsteps of the nineteenth-century nationalist Jules Michelet. In antithesis to Hobsbawm's Marxist suspicions about nationalist historians, Braudel maintained that the discipline of history was best staffed by adepts of the nation: 'The historian can really be on equal footing only with the history of his own country; he understands almost instinctively its twists and turns, its complexities, its originalities and its weaknesses.'[8] France, Braudel contended, tumbling into deep waters for a man who had opposed Nazism, did not start with the Revolution of 1789. Rather, it was born in 'pre-Roman Gaul', in village construction and 'blood groups'. With regard to the 'outside world', Braudel added with an eager dismissal of centuries of movement of different peoples across French territory, 'there may be some intermingling but there is no fusion'.

It is true that, later in his book, Braudel did acknowledge that 'France is not one society . . . but many societies.' Yet, he remained convinced that each diversity slotted neatly into a greater unity. No one invented France; rather, the nation was 'of its own making' and, in this creative process, 'the crucial events

> *No one invented France;
> rather, the nation was
> 'of its own making'*

occurred in fact millennia ago'.[9] For Braudel, the immigrants who had entered the country in vast numbers in his own lifetime carried no real history, or none that could last. They had to assimilate, to merge with France, rather than having the nation merge with them.

The Croat Adam

Even in the allegedly more restrained western European nations, places where nationalism is frequently presented as measured and composed, it is clear that a fervent discourse has flourished into the most recent times, urging that the sense of national belonging is old, not new. To the east, still more grandiose claims about national ubiquity and longevity are everywhere apparent. To give but one example, a Croatian historian in North American exile from communist Yugoslavia in the 1970s, trying to be modest with evident difficulty, urged that 'the Croatians are one of the ancient peoples, not only of Europe, but perhaps of the entire world'. Paying no attention to the fact that the word 'Croat' did not appear until the tenth century and then was uncertain in meaning,[10] he declared unconvincingly that 'it can be stated with authority that the Croatians, at the time when they enter history in Media and Persia and earlier, were already a people with their own state organization, and thus a developed idea of the state . . . This idea of state made it possible for them to preserve their state unity through many millennia, through many events and vicissitudes, through continents and many migrations.' All in all, then, Croats, he pronounced, were 'one of the oldest cultural peoples of Europe, and a people who constantly remained independent from pre-Aryan times, thus about two millennia before Christ, until our own times'.[11]

Eternity questioned

According to several analysts, then, current identity is profoundly rooted in ancient origins. Yet there are plenty of reasons to doubt this assertion. Erasmus's text, after all, points in two directions. In the third millennium, we may still be ready to admit French intellectual achievement or arrogance, Greek pretensions to a long history, Jewish and Muslim faith and Italian fondness for rhetoric. But is it an automatic given that the 'British' [sic] are natural leaders in music and cuisine, the Germans in magic, the Scots in monarchism and formality? If, it must be asked, the so-called 'core values' of a nation change over time, as, given the constant flux of the human condition, they do, does the nation remain the nation? It is similarly a worry that, in the mind's eye of Erasmus, the nations are composed of men (women do not rate a mention). And what of the eliding of nation and city? Would Erasmus have conceded that the peasants of Italy held different belief systems from those of the citizenry of Rome or Venice? In this perspective, so far from the populism that frequently characterizes modern nationalism and anxiously unearths reality in country life, were rural dwellers and illiterates not implicitly to be written off in the listing of national character as 'barbarians and riff-raff', people who, like all non-Europeans, did not matter? Yet, if the attitudes and behaviour of the nation are different from one region of its rule to another, can it really be accepted as a timeless single entity?

What, too, of Erasmus's uneasy drift from definitions based on 'nation' to stereotypes based on religion? Was he endorsing the view, preached by the Zionists of present times, that the Jews constituted a nation through the two millennia when no 'Jewish state' existed? But if so, what was he implying about 'Turks', seemingly his shorthand for Muslims, and certainly extending beyond the subjects of the Ottoman Empire and 'Sublime Porte'? The more the generalizations penned by Erasmus are studied, the more problematic they become. His statement illuminates the fact that he and others, at the beginning of the sixteenth century in Europe, believed that human beings were not always the same and were willing to categorize some of the variation as prompted by geography, history, language, culture and the presence or otherwise of a state. It can thus be agreed that, before the Enlightenment and French Revolution drastically shook the ordering of society and then looked to a new and scientific precision as the basis of modernity, streams of some sort of ethnicity may have existed that were eventually channelled into nationality. But they were not alone or by any means dominant. In so far as people's identities are concerned, the pre-modern world is full of other tides, currents that were destined not to sway the future but rather to be obscured or destroyed by it.

The multicultural empire: Rome

Empires have been a recurring feature of human history. Rome dominated Europe for six centuries, China overawed east Asia for three millennia and there were plenty more fleeting imitators. Each empire had recourse to ideology to mould its peoples and, like the nationalists of our own times, was happy to add history to the quiver of weapons through which it ruled. Yet the pre-modern empires were scarcely nations in the making. Rome, with such figures as Livy and Tacitus, may have sponsored in its early empire historians who talked about the *natio* or *nationes* and even, on occasion, used the term for the Romans. It is unlikely, however, that its meaning was national in any modern sense. The 'Greek' 'Father of History' (and anthropology) Herodotus, in his description of an ancient world, chopped up peoples geographically and culturally but provided no lasting explanation of the variations between them, and certainly not a racial or a cultural one.[12] In any case, Herodotus's Greekness displays something of the linguistic and cultural variety of the Roman Empire, where he was still treasured and read. For centuries, Latin and Greek cohabited in this realm, and the test of a civilized man (women were rarely thus categorized) was often that he must have mastered both languages and, more importantly, know when and where each was to be used. Militarily, the story is also erratic. When they conquered Dacia, the Romans do seem to have assimilated the population linguistically; certainly they left behind a Latinate language in what was to become Romania. In Britain, however, the poorer social groups did not adopt Latin.[13]

For all the conquests achieved by its legions, Rome remained philosophically a backward-looking society, with its elites typically finding the empire, even at the pinnacle of its power, inadequate or in decay. In their minds, it was both eternal and under constant threat of dissolution. It was also in some sense, even at its most boundless, a city state, with a citizenship that, when it was extended across the Italian peninsula, continued to be based in the various cities. Eventually, the brutal and short-lived

Emperor Caracalla, himself from a family with a background in Syria and Africa, granted citizenship to all free men throughout the vast territories under his rule in 212 AD. This step, taken at a time when tax receipts were proving inadequate, religious division was increasing and the social gap between rich and poor, landowners and tenants, was growing, despite the Severan dynasty's favouring of egalitarian rhetoric, made Romanness universal, at least in theory. Such an empire was plainly not the site of nations or proto-nations and when, in the 260s, a Gallic breakaway realm flourished for some years, its institutional and ideological base remained generically Roman and not something looking for its identity specifically to Gaul.[14]

The splits between the experience of the free and the slave, and between men and women, were other fundamental features of Roman life radically different from modern experience. The fate of slaves was not nationalized, given that they could be freed, and at no time during Roman rule were they inscribed with a 'clear-cut racial, ethnic or religious boundary', nor with a linguistic one.[15] Perhaps the most consistent division in Rome, and one replicated in China and quite a few other imperial societies, was the binary view that the empire was under permanent siege by outsiders, by people damned as 'barbarians'. Some could be converted into Romans after settlement and military service, but they would only be succeeded by more barbarians, peoples who, unlike Romans, were allegedly not possessed of a history.[16] Ancient empires were in some part killing machines and, despite the common civil wars, most of those massacred were barbarians outside the law and outside the reckoning of Rome, outside humanity. The Roman realm, in other words, split the world in two. It was characterized and always would be by an 'Us' and an othered 'Them'; in this image, there was no glimmer of the modern representation of the world as constituted by a multiplicity of nations, where, in positive vein, humankind might

The Roman realm split the world in two. It was characterized and always would be by an 'Us' and an othered 'Them'

be able to rejoice in its own colour and variety.

The multicultural empire: China

The Chinese Empire, in its successive dynastic and sometimes ethnically diverse manifestations, replicated quite a few of these ideas and this behaviour. The realm lasted so long that the language of administration and of its carefully trained bureaucrats or mandarins could act both to hold together peoples of very different tongues, religions and cultures and, eventually, to provide the basis of China's dominant, if by no means single, language today. The idea of accurate classification and of the clear-cut border, in Europe such a part of the Enlightenment and the 'scientific revolution' and so much an unspoken assumption of the contemporaneous rise of nationalism, can be detected in China ages before. 'In no other part of the world', it has been remarked, was 'the decimalisation of weights and measures so early and so consistent'[17]; the issue had been thought through in the third century BC. Similarly, a lingering argument surfaced from time to time in political and proto-political circles during the 268-year rule of the Manchu Dynasty down to 1911 that its emperors were somehow 'foreign'. Yet the twentieth-century appearance of Chinese 'nationalism' was a modern idea, seeping in from Europe. It was bolstered by the resentment of European imperialists,

Chinese 'nationalism' was a modern idea, seeping in from Europe. It was bolstered by the resentment of European imperialists, with their own ignorant and ruthless interference in the Chinese imperium, economy and culture, and by hostility towards the Japanese indulgence in similar behaviour

with their own ignorant and ruthless interference in the Chinese imperium, economy and culture, and by hostility towards the Japanese indulgence in similar behaviour, as, for example, was made manifest in the wartime 'Twenty-One Demands' of December 1915.[18] Even then, the typical inhabitant of the Chinese realm, whether imperial, nationalist or communist, was illiterate and in cultural terms a world away from those elites who set the country's borders and worried about their infraction.[19]

Other empires

In their eager hunt for 'great men' in the past who could give posthumous lustre to those who presently aspire either to be great or to be celebrated, present-day nations have carelessly raised many conquerors of fleeting empires to the status of 'heroes of the nation', ruthlessly wrenching history awry in the process. Justified by the fact that Tamerlane or Timur the Lame (1336–1405) had a capital for a while at Samarkand, modern Uzbekistan is told that he was its forebear. Tamerlane is credited with ruling over the most extensive empire the world has ever seen, although, after his death, it was soon prey to the rivalry of his sons and other heirs. Mongolia salutes the grandeur that emanated from his probable ancestor, Genghis Khan

(c. 1162–1227). The main airport in Ulaanbaatar is named after him and there are some suggestions that the post-communist country should be renamed 'Genghis Mongolia', an appellation that, if it were to succeed, would push to a new extreme the habit of nations to revere their war dead and to forget those whom their soldiers killed. For what might be thought more sophisticated sponsors and audience, a semi-official exhibition on 'Turks: a journey of a thousand years, 600–1600', held in London in 2005 and given official endorsement by prime ministers Tony Blair and Tayyip Erdogan, cheerfully annexed both Tamerlane and Genghis Khan to a Turkish imperial past. The two conquerors' posthumous charisma was meant to add impulse to the current Turkish nation state's hope to be admitted to 'Europe'.[20]

The identity of the stateless

Contemporary manipulation or misunderstanding of the past should not lead anyone to join the Romans in assuming that 'barbarians', who failed to assemble in literate pre-modern empires, did not actually live in complex, varied and changing societies. Modern anthropology is another subject that cemented its authority as a discipline in the university at the same moment that nations came into political being. Perhaps even more than historians, anthropologists have had a deplorable record of time-serving, often grovellingly telling their governments and paymasters what they wanted to hear. Yet, at their best, anthropologists have fostered a humble comprehension of how complex and textured 'pre-modern' societies are and always have been. It may be tempting to agree that historians waste their time when they try to uncover from illiterate societies too clear an evidential base of popular yearning and identity,[21] and yet social groups lacking much in the way of their own literature and written histories do not deserve to be ignored in any analysis of nationalism.

The prime point to make is that, throughout the history of humankind, areas being 'governed' were much more likely to be fluid, polyglot and 'multicultural' than to be confined to a coherent, timeless and homogeneous nationality or identity. Perhaps peasant mountain villagers, be they in Europe or Irian Jaya, could, on occasion and for a time, live outside the 'rage of history'. For the rest of humankind, the world was always a textured place, where priests, soldiers, prostitutes, students and those with one skill or another were seldom geographically confined throughout their lives. In this shifting scene, language, behaviour and sense of self or family were open to negotiation in some fashion. As the courageous contemporary Turkish novelist Orhan Pamuk has tried to explain (thus risking his acceptance as a loyal 'Turkish national writer'), Istanbul, until the twentieth century, was less 'the nation's capital', zealously recalling its foundation in the overthrow of Byzantium in 1453, and more a place of multiple meanings where, at its simplest, half the population was 'Greek'.[22]

The historian Mark Mazower, in his tracking of the story of Salonica/Thessaloniki just across the Aegean Sea, concurs. In his eyes, this city is now stalked by the 'ghosts' of the many

> *The world was always a textured place, where priests, soldiers, prostitutes, students and those with one skill or another were seldom geographically confined throughout their lives*

peoples and their disjointed pasts expunged in the process of Greek nationalization. As late as 1910, Mazower reports, there were still 10 000 *Ma'mins*, a Judaeo-Spanish-speaking group of highly independent Muslims who owed their origins to a converted Jewish millenarian of the seventeenth century, Sabbatai Zevi. Following the brutal Balkan wars in 1912–13 and their accompanying outbursts of ethnic cleansing, the *Ma'mins* and many similar peoples disappeared, with Mazower left to complain: 'The history of the nationalists is all about false continuities and convenient silences, the fictions necessary to tell the story of the rendez-vous of a chosen people with the land marked out for them by destiny.'[23]

Any excursion into the social character of the past lays bare myriad further examples of human heterogeneity and the intricacy with which webs of human beings coexisted more or less successfully before they were forced to confront the modern demand for homogeneity. In this regard, the historian Yuri Slezkine, with a degree of bravado, has split the world into 'Apollonians' (those who stayed at home) and 'Mercurians', the travellers and specialists, needed by, and found in, every society. His list of the latter is long:

In medieval Korea, the Koli such'ok and Hwach.ok-chaein people were employed as basket weavers, shoemakers, hunters, butchers, sorcerers, torturers, border guards, buffoons, dancers, and puppeteers. In Ashikaga and Tokugawa Japan, the Eta specialized in animal slaughter, public executions, and mortuary services, and the Hinin monopolized begging, prostitution, juggling, dog training, and snake charming. In early twentieth-century Africa, the Yibir practiced magic, surgery, and leatherwork among the Somalis; the Fuga of southern Ethiopia were

ritual experts and entertainers as well as wood carvers and potters;
and throughout the Sahel, Sahara, and Sudan, travelling blacksmiths
often doubled as cattle dealers, circumcisers, peddlers, jewellers,
musicians, and conflict mediators. In Europe, various 'Gypsy' and
'Traveler' groups specialized in tinsmithing, knife sharpening, chimney
sweeping, horse dealing, fortune-telling, jewelry making, itinerant
trading, entertainment, and scavenging (including begging, stealing,
and the collection of scrap metal and used clothing for resale).[24]

This rich agglomeration by no means exhausts those who fall
into this category. The most evident 'service nomads', Slezkine
asserts, were the Jews, with their fellows being 'Parsis,
Armenians, Eastern European Germans, Overseas Indians and
Overseas Chinese'.[25] None of these people fitted tidily into a
world hammered into separate nation states. It may be a cliché
that, of ancient peoples, the Jews went closest to being a modern
nation,[26] but, ironically, the devotion of Jews to certain activities
and the identity that resulted thereby were enhanced once the
state of Israel had been destroyed by the Romans and the Jews
had been dispersed. If they were a proto-nation, then they were
one that by definition lacked set frontiers (and so omitted the
first principle of the modern nation state). Slezkine summarizes
the dilemma with brilliant and challenging wit:

The principal religion of the Modern Age is nationalism, a faith that
represents the new society as the old community and allows newly
urbanized princes and peasants to feel at home abroad. Every state
must have a tribe; every tribe must have a state. Every language is
Adamic, every capital Jerusalem, and every people chosen (and ancient).
The Age of Nationalism, in other words, is about every nation becoming
Jewish. [Yet,] in nineteenth-century Europe, . . . the greatest exception

was the Jews themselves . . . The greatest beneficiaries of the Age of Capitalism, they would become the greatest victims of the Age of Nationalism. More desperate than any other European nation for state protection, they were the least likely to receive it because no European nation-state could possibly claim to be the embodiment of the Jewish nation.[27]

The troubled relationship between the Jews and the nation will continue to be a theme of this book. But the point is made that, before the onset of modernity, societies brimmed with peoples whose clothes, occupations, religions, tongues, marriage practices, habits in preparing and consuming food and even their body odour distinguished them from settled majorities.

> *Societies brimmed with peoples whose clothes, occupations, religions, tongues, marriage practices, habits in preparing and consuming food and even their body odour distinguished them from settled majorities*

The moving border

In most senses, the modern frontier was another invention of the Enlightenment – the social scientist Ernest Gellner handily defined the nation as 'a bordered power-container'[28] – and the bearing of national passports by individuals did not become automatic until the twentieth century. Even then, confusion and incomprehension could reign: one independent-minded Russian visitor managed to enter pre-1914 Australia by showing customs officials in Brisbane an old theatre programme printed in Cyrillic script and so a portentously foreign language.[29] For the great majority of pre-modern states, by contrast, borders were fluctuating sites, depending for their placement on the latest military incursion, attacks that were as natural a part of spring and summer as were the precarious growth and harvesting of crops. Where the frontier was especially significant and contested – in Europe, notably in the Balkans, where the Christian and Muslim worlds abutted once the forces of the Ottoman Empire penetrated beyond the Straits in the fifteenth century, or for many centuries before that in Spain – it may be that a special frontier mentality developed. The border sometimes allowed entrepreneurial adaptation to rival cultures; on other occasions, it was neurotically emphatic about difference and ready to murder and lay waste in order to impose a brief but desired uniformity and settlement. One ramification may have been a 'hostile mimickery' that spread the idea of eternal difference between the contending parties.[30] But another was a willingness to trade and converse and an emotional separation of those who lived on the frontier from more sedentary people.

The exception might seem the proto-states of England, France and some of the other eventual nations of western Europe.[31] As has been noted, nationalist historians are eager to assert that these societies did possess real frontiers, and ones that were understood as sundering one people from another; John of Gaunt's already cited 'precious stone set in a silver sea' might seem to be proof. Yet, in medieval and early modern England, was the international frontier washed by the surrounding seas really the only one to exist? Were there not plenty of borders, albeit contested ones, between this part of the country and that? Loyalty to the local notable remained powerful and basic to most

'Englishmen' and women. It was said, 'even in Tudor times', that the northern counties of the land 'had never known a king other than a Percy, a Howard or a Dacre'. Under Edward IV (1461–83), who was quite successful in imposing his rule, a commentator stated that the Percy Earls of Northumberland 'have the hearts of the people by north and ever had'.[32] Popular identity, in other words, sprang as much from the people's service to their lord as it did to any notion of being English. The constancy in such societies of civil broils should also not be underestimated. It has been argued that one of the key elements in the formation of proto-nations is the neighbour–enemy, fought over and over again in wars where patriotic evocations become the norm; England and France may have been constituted in this way during the Hundred Years' War.[33] Yet part of this conflict's fame was constructed by nationalist and nationalizing historians in the nineteenth century, and any full tabulation of violent conflict involving the subjects of the kings of England and France through the Middle Ages would scarcely place at its centre war between the two.

Pre-modern warriors fought because there was no help for it or because they were paid to do so, either directly or in the opportunity to sack a town, to rape and pillage. The switch to a more moralized soldiering occurred slowly and partially. One of the great changes of the French Revolution was national conscription and the replacement of the mercenary soldier or sailor with one who fought selflessly for the nation. Such attitudes were not adopted fully in the Russian armies by 1914, let alone by those who then went into battle in extra-European states. Without them, the relationship of war and the people was scarcely nationalized. (Nationalized battle cannot be assumed to be nicer. As William Calley explained his platoon's appalling deeds at My Lai in Vietnam: 'Personally I didn't kill any Vietnamese that day: I mean personally. I represented the United States of America. My country.'[34])

Eighteenth-century forgings

The most convincing view is that 'Britons' were only forged, and then not universally so in the 'United Kingdom' after the constitutional fusing of the kingdoms of England and Scotland in 1707. To the dismay of patriotic conservatives, sure that 'Britain was not invented; it grew',[35] critical historians have argued that the concept of 'Great Britain' arose through war and the commitment to Protestantism and through such more general factors as demographic change (more young), the availability of the first newspapers, and the improvement of roads and other sinews of communication.[36] By contrast:

Great Britain in 1707 was much less a trinity of three self-contained and self-conscious nations than a patchwork of uncertain areas of Welshness, Scottishness and Englishness, cut across by strong regional attachments, and scored over again by loyalties to village, town, family and landscape. In other words, like virtually every other part of Europe in this period, Great Britain was markedly diverse in terms of the customs and cultures of its inhabitants.[37]

A century later, the process of building a new loyalty and commitment and a new sense of identity had acquired fresh momentum. When calling on volunteers to fight Napoleon and 'revolution', prime minister William Pitt remarked that: 'There was a time when it would have been dangerous to entrust arms with a great proportion of the people of this country . . . But that time is now past.' And those enrolled to fight came 'from all social classes, all religious denominations and all political opinions', as well as from all parts of the country.[38] In part qualifying the leftist historian E.P. Thompson's (patriotic) claim that the Augustan age was seeing the self-making of the English working class,[39] Linda Colley, the most acute commentator in the field, has urged instead that it was British patriots who were 'present at their own birth' and who were destined thereafter to condition the British experience of empire and power. In this Britishness, they were also downplaying, at least for a time, those potential identities that might have as readily been nationalized as English, Scottish, Welsh and Irish.

In a later study, Colley has acknowledged that, through the eighteenth century, Europeans were simultaneously capable of 'crossing over' into what today would be called developing-world societies and there, if their stay was extended and they found some form of *sistemazione*, assimilating themselves to the non-European other.[40] As such adaptability demonstrates, the uneven and still potentially transient making of Britishness in the eighteenth century bears comparison with the attempts in Germany and Italy to nationalize their populations, after the formation of the two new nation states with those names in the second half of the nineteenth century.

Again an irony shines through the historical narrative. If Britons were being made in the eighteenth century out of erstwhile proto-English and the rest, what was happening in France, a country that had not been fused with another, as England was with Scotland, since the French acquisition of Brittany and some of the Languedoc at the end of the Middle Ages? Enlightenment intellectuals, the framers of the encyclopaedia, are often depicted as the key forces in demanding that modernity classify and differentiate peoples just as modernity itself was to do with anything that could be exposed to 'scientific' examination. But, even in France, the situation lacked simplicity. Among the *philosophes*, Voltaire, for one, was willing to state that the French were 'an assemblage of Goths, Danes, Germans, Franks, Swiss and some Romans mixed with old Celts'. In any case, debates about what might today be deemed national identity had to take a back seat to 'politics' as Rousseau, himself perhaps Swiss, was ready to proclaim. The French, too, had not yet been made in 1789.[41]

In sum, the idea that nations had already come into existence before the eighteenth century and that a rich humus of potential nationality lay around in most societies seems exaggerated. As one critical commentator has noted wryly: 'There are usually several different nationalisms which claim to represent the same nation at the same time' and each will find its justification in history.[42] More telling is the fact that, given the frequent underestimation of the complexity and heterogeneity of pre-modern societies, riven as they were with class, gender, ethnic, age, regional, religious, occupational and many other differences, to map a highway leading to a national present and future inevitably conceals all the other tracks then in existence but ones that did not naturally debouch into the nation. Nationalism and nations were to be born together in the Enlightenment and in the French and Industrial revolutions. The constancy and stridency of their appeals

Nationalism and nations were to be born together in the Enlightenment and in the French and Industrial revolutions

to history were not based entirely on cynical invention. Yet nationalized histories were everywhere made uniform and uni-linear in a way that insults and demeans the uncertainty and variation of the human story. In framing national myths around ancient pasts, nationalists have hidden the actual story of 'constant change, of radical discontinuities, and of political and cultural zigzags masked by the repeated re-appropriation of old words to define new realities'.[43] The nationalists are not even original in their determination to claim a past for themselves and deny it to others. Forging usable history is what all humans do and always have done.

Notes

1　D. Erasmus, *Praise of Folly and Letter to Martin Dorp 1515* (ed. A.H.T. Levi) (1971, Harmondsworth: Penguin), pp. 132–3.

2　A.D. Smith, *The Ethnic Origins of Nations* (1986, Oxford: Basil Blackwell), p. ix.

3　C. Allmand, *Henry V* (1999, New Haven, CT: Yale University Press), pp. xix, 407.

4　*Ibid.* pp. 13, 406.

5　J. Gillingham, *Richard I* (1999, New Haven, CT: Yale University Press), p. 9.

6　R.R. Davies, *The First English Empire: Power and Identities in the British Isles 1093–1343* (2000, Oxford: Oxford University Press), pp. 41, 50, 123, 201.

7　For an argument of this case, see R.J.B. Bosworth, *Explaining Auschwitz and Hiroshima: History Writing and the Second World War 1945–1990* (1993, London: Routledge), pp. 94–117.

8　F. Braudel, *The Identity of France, vol. I: History and Environment* (1988, London: Fontana), pp. 15, 19–20.

9   *Ibid.* pp. 72, 126, 305.

10 P.J. Geary, *The Myth of Nations: The Medieval Origins of Europe* (2002, Princeton, NJ: Princeton University Press), p. 148.

11 I. Omrcanin, *Diplomatic and Political History of Croatia* (1972, Philadelphia, PA: Dorrance), pp. 1, 32, 181.

12 Geary, *The Myth of Nations*, pp. 43–6.

13 J. Bennett, *Trajan: Optimus Princeps: A Life and Times* (1997, London: Routledge), p. 172.

14 A. Watson, *Aurelian and the Third Century* (1999, London: Routledge), p. 100.

15 Geary, *The Myth of Nations*, p. 65.

16 *Ibid.* p. 50.

17 J. Needham, *Science and Civilisation in China*, vol. IV (1962, Cambridge: Cambridge University Press) p. 43.

18 I.C.Y. Hsü, *The Rise of Modern China* (1970, Hong Kong: Oxford University Press), pp. 494–5.

19 As emphasized by Eric Hobsbawm in *Nations and Nationalism since 1780: Programme, Myth, Reality* (1990, Cambridge: Cambridge University Press), p. 62.

20 D.J. Roxburgh, *Turks: A Journey of a Thousand Years, 600–1600* (2005, London: Royal Academy of Arts).

21 J. Breuilly, *Nationalism and the State* (rev. edn) (1991, Manchester: Manchester University Press), p. 401.

22 O. Pamuk, *Istanbul: Memories of a City* (2005, New York: Alfred Knopf), p. 157.

23 M. Mazower, *Salonica: City of Ghosts: Christians, Muslims and Jews 1430–1950* (2004, London: Harper Collins), pp. 71–5, 474.

24 Y. Slezkine, *The Jewish Century* (2004, Princeton, NJ: Princeton University Press), pp. 4–5.

25 *Ibid.* p. 29.

26 For one endorsement, see A.D. Smith, *National Identity* (1991, Harmondsworth: Penguin), p. 50.

27 Slezkine, *The Jewish Century*, pp. 1–2.

28 Cited by J. Hutchinson and A.D. Smith (eds) *Nationalism* (1994, Oxford: Oxford University Press), p. 34.

29 J. Wilton and R. Bosworth, *Old Worlds and New Australia: The Post-War Migrant Experience* (1984, Ringwood: Penguin), p. 42.

30 J.A. Armstrong, *Nations before Nationalism* (1982, Chapel Hill, NC: University of North Carolina Press), p. 91.

31 Smith, *National Identity*, p. 59 adds Spain, Sweden and Holland to this list.

32 C. Ross, *Edward IV* (1997, New Haven, CT: Yale University Press), p. 393.

33 Smith, *National Identity*, p. 27.

34 Cited by J. Bourke, *An Intimate History of Killing: Face-to-Face Killing in Twentieth Century Warfare* (1999, London: Granta Books), p. 236.

35 J.C.D. Clark, 'Protestantism, nationalism, and national identity, 1660–1832', *Historical Journal*, 2000, 43, p. 275.

36 For her summary, see L. Colley, 'Whose nation? Class and national consciousness in Britain 1750–1830', *Past and Present*, 1986, 113, pp. 100–104.

37 L. Colley, *Britons: Forging the Nation 1707–1837* (1994, London: Pimlico), p. 17.

38 *Ibid.* pp. 310, 317.

39 E.P. Thompson, *The Making of the English Working Class* (1968, Harmondsworth: Penguin).

40 See L. Colley, 'Going native, telling tales: captivity, collaborations and empire', *Past and Present*, 2000, 168, pp. 170–193; *Captives: Britain, Empire and the World, 1600–1850* (2003, London: Pimlico).

41 D.A. Bell, 'Lingua popoli, lingua dei: language, religion, and the origins of French revolutionary nationalism', *American Historical Review*, 1995, 100, pp. 1225–7.

42 E. Benner, *Really Existing Nationalism: A Post Communist View from Marx and Engels* (1995, Oxford: Clarendon), p. 8.

43 Geary, *The Myth of Nations*, p. 157.

CHAPTER 3

Nation, nationalism and revolution 1789–1914

'*LIBERTÉ, EGALITÉ, FRATERNITÉ*', the great motto of the French Revolution, originally with the menacingly activist addition of '*ou la mort*' (Freedom, Equality, Fraternity or death), has echoed through subsequent history. The French were still arguing about what the words had entailed, or should entail, in 1989, during the Revolution's bicentenary. Then, advancing neo-conservatives proclaimed that the Revolution was at last over, since, they maintained, liberty and equality had become 'common currency' (fraternity was ignored). With the approach of the new millennium, all could accept that '1789 was good, 1793 [the period of Jacobin "terrorism"] was bad'. Moreover, French exceptionalism had also come to rest: 'Politics was now less about ideology than about management', they affirmed, and France, just another western liberal democratic nation, was preparing itself cosily to enjoy the 'end of history'.[1]

1789 and all that

The process of history since the Enlightenment can be read as a contest between the desire to be free, the desire to be equal and the desire to base the state on popular sovereignty and thereafter to live in love and charity with the nation's neighbours

The arrogance and blindness of the neo-conservative reckoing with modernity may be left to its own devices. But, certainly, the process of history since the Enlightenment can be read as a contest between the desire to be free, the desire to be equal and the desire to base the state on popular sovereignty and thereafter to live in love and charity with the nation's neighbours. From *liberté* liberalism; from *egalité* socialism; from *fraternité* nationalism. Yet, despite the bliss of the revolutionary prospect that men and women were about to be made anew, in the longer term, for humankind the modern trinity entailed an inescapable dilemma. During the next two centuries, some advantages and endless difficulties were to result from the thoughts and actions of those who sought to be liberals and nationalists but not socialists, nationalists and socialists but not liberals, liberals and socialists but not nationalists, and from the other juddering encounters of each of these groups.

What, after all, were women to make of the sexist word 'fraternity'? It may be that, in 1789, French women shared the widespread desire to 'become a nation', with a peddler crying her wares as 'national plums, national apples'. Maybe identity formation within the family had long rested more in female than male hands; as a contemporary writer put it: 'men make the laws but women make *moeurs*, there lies their true empire'.[2] Yet, as modern feminists have taken pains to explain, the French Revolution scarcely delivered female liberation. 'Marianne', the icon of the revolutionary nation, may have been portrayed as female and Mary Wollstonecraft in Britain may have been spurred by the news from France to vindicate the rights of women.[3] By 1796, however, whatever had been the initial hope in social, economic and gender freedom, the women of France had 'ended up on their knees'.[4] In Le Puy, they signalled their rejection of the Revolution by clawing imprisoned local Jacobin leaders to death before marching defiantly through the town to reopen the Church.[5] The female nurturers of family identity had not yet embraced the national family, it was clear.

One reason for women's sorrow, even at this early stage of the world order's efforts to cope with the revolutionary nation, was endless and ubiquitous conflict. The commonest later summary of the European experience from 1789 to 1815 was 'the era of revolutionary war'. The Rights of Man [sic] may have proclaimed that 'men are born and remain free and equal in rights' and that 'the source of all sovereignty is essentially in the nation; no body, no individual, can exercise authority that does not proceed from it'.[6] But many treacherous currents swirled through the fine print of what these phrases might mean and how their meaning could be adjusted to the victories of the French Revolutionary forces and their allies and, eventually, their defeat and overthrow.

Warring the nation (part one)

A recent study of French behaviour in the Italian states after 1796 has concluded that, despite Napoleon Bonaparte's jaunty

Jules Michelet

One of the great books of the nineteenth century was *Histoire de France* (*History of France*), published in 17 volumes between 1833 and 1867 (in the 1890s a revised edition spread to 40 volumes) and written by Jules Michelet.

Michelet was born in 1798, the son of a Parisian printer, the follower of a trade that had played a prominent part in the revolution of 1789 and after. Michelet remained a lifelong republican through the vicissitudes of French politics until his death in 1874. He was educated in Paris and soon made a mark as a historian, writing on a huge span of topics and eras and filling a number of professorial positions (in 1851, he had to step down from one after he refused to take an oath to Napoleon III's 'Second Empire').

Michelet's history-writing was always sparked by an overt political purpose. 'To reproduce so many passions', he would write as he combed the past for meaning, was 'not to calm one's own'. Committed to archival research and going well beyond such predecessors as that European-wide celebrity, the historical novelist Walter Scott, Michelet, for all his present commitment, was sure that 'the souls of our fathers still throb in us for the pains that have been forgotten'. Michelet knew that France had a mission to lead 'Europe' and was convinced that significant political remedies were always trialled first in his country. Among his stars in the past was Joan of Arc, 'the Virgin descended to earth', as he phrased it, the fervently spiritual embodiment of the people's thirst for freedom and independence.

Almost in spite of himself, Michelet was therefore privileging the nation over other positive aspects of the Great Revolution where, he was certain, 'the principal actor' was 'the people' and the principal aim 'profoundly pacific [and] benevolent'. Simultaneously, Michelet introduced himself into his own narrative in an almost post-modern manner. As an American journalist commented sardonically: 'We are not surprised when, arriving at last at the year 1798, we find Michelet's own birth recorded as an event to which all that had gone before from the Merovingian and Carolingian dynasties has in some sense been leading up.'[7] In regard to France's relationship with the wider world, Michelet had continued to treat *fraternité* as a good and natural ambition of the best of the revolutionaries, detecting no contradiction in French 'leadership' and the often in fact hostile foreign reaction to the arrival in their societies of revolutionary and then Napoleonic armies.

Michelet was an ardent advocate of the view that Napoleon was a 'destroyer' of the Revolution on the less than strictly fraternal grounds that he was an alien, uncomprehending of the real France. In old age, Michelet was appalled by the events of 1870–71, brought on by 'Napoleon the little'. Initially Michelet joined with Marx and Engels in endorsing a pacifist line towards the war between France and Bismarck's German confederation. French defeat, however, stung him, and he wrote emotionally of the need for an 'armed peace league' of 'the labouring, the industrious' to repel the advance of Prussian militarism. When France collapsed into further revolution and civil war during the Commune, Michelet was paralysed by a series of strokes, leaving the last volumes of his great history to come out posthumously. The spirit of his invention of the French nation would, however, remain powerful for many years. Fernand Braudel was not alone in thinking of him as 'unrivalled' among France's historians.

claim that the invading armies and the administrators who followed them had 'no other end than to oversee, guarantee and advance the national education of Italians', the reality was that the French engaged in brutal and aggressive 'cultural imperialism' in Italy.[8] Locals were viewed as irredeemably 'other'. Ignorant in the extreme, the invaders and occupiers jostled existing patron–client networks, factional disputes and cultural values violently and, for the most part, unpredictably, even if 'Madonnas proved themselves to be [counter-] revolutionary activists all over Italy'.[9] The result was popular counter-revolution that, going beyond mere reaction, promised further trouble for the alliance of freedom, equality and fraternity.

What happened in Italy was repeated in the rest of Europe, as rival armies marched across political and social, formal and informal, borders and, in the process, either erased them or pushed them massively awry. Among the perpetrators of armed revolution and modernity at the bloody bayonet's point was Napoleon Bonaparte, the epitome of revolutionary hope or aspiration, the ruler whom German polymath J.W. Goethe would recall as the greatest in history, a 'demigod . . . in a state of continual illumination'.[10] This thrusting everyman was born in peripheral Corsica, remaining in quite a few senses an 'amoral familist'. Yet, 'free' indeed, he rose from humble obscurity to be a military conqueror, emperor of France, and a ruler who could allegedly boast that 'a man like me troubles little about the lives of millions'.[11]

When asked whether Napoleon was the 'prophet of the modern [nation] state', historians reply that the key to his personality lay in the mathematical quickness and accuracy he displayed as a junior officer and his preference as a ruler for 'uniformity, symmetry and efficiency'.[12] It may be more perceptive to write off both Napoleon and his nephew, Napoleon III, emperor of France from 1849 to 1870, as members of a 'gangster dynasty',[13] mafiosi who had grabbed state power. Yet Napoleon's belief that enumeration and computation could resolve the world did, at the same time and with whatever contradiction, express Enlightenment rationality and the belief of the age that God was dead and human perfection was possible. When, at Napoleon's nod, the borders of Europe were overridden by revolutionary armies, the presumption survived thereafter that, somehow drawn more expertly and neatly, made to express a more genuine popular sovereignty, welcoming each of the diverse nations in their pomp and glory, new frontiers could be fashioned to guarantee perpetual peace and universal human happiness. The trick for intelligent statesmen from Napoleon to US president Woodrow Wilson in 1919 and beyond was to locate the ideal formula to permit a world of nations. And reinforcing the scheming of politicians was, or seemed to be, the popular will, since the majority of humans were more ready to rally behind the nation than to devote themselves to securing freedom or equality.

> *Reinforcing the scheming of politicians was the popular will, since the majority of humans were more ready to rally behind the nation than to devote themselves to securing freedom or equality*

Thinking the nation

The Enlightenment had seen the birth of the modern intelligentsia, half opportunist Figaros and half cultivated *philosophes*. Quick to map the process through which the nations could be cemented into place were a slew of philosophers, led by Johann Gottfried von Herder (1744–1803), a man who rose to be Prussian court preacher from the 1770s and whose somewhat rambling *Ideen zur Philosophie der Geschichte der Menscheit* (*Reflections on the Philosophy of the History of Mankind*) (1784–91) became highly influential in its sketching of the lineaments of the nation. Prussia, after all, was on the march, first in opposing Napoleonic invasion between 1806 and 1813 and later in harnessing the movement towards German unification. For Herder, good and evil, civilization and murder, battled for 'man', as he phrased it. There were grounds for optimism in this epic contest: 'Peace . . . not war is the natural state of mankind when at liberty'. 'War', Herder preached, was 'the offspring of necessity, not the legitimate child of enjoyment'. 'God', he reasoned in words to be applauded by many romantics during the following decades, was deeply inscribed into the beauties of 'nature' and into the more Spartan sphere of 'history'. 'Man's' 'history, like that of the grub,' he wrote with an attempt at wit, 'is intimately interwoven with that of the web which he inhabits.' Since humans were 'a diverging species', the new task was to locate and to foster each nation, thus allowing the expression of its special and copious individuality, even while remaining alert to the fact that 'nations modify themselves according to time, place, and their internal character'.[14] Scarcely himself a revolutionary, Herder was endorsing the claim of the French Encyclopaedia in 1752 that 'each nation has its own character'[15] and prophesying the triumph of peace and love in a world of nations.

The Restoration and its national discontents

In 1815, then, with Napoleon confined to St Helena and reduced to the irksome task of composing his own story as that of a modest and virtuous heir and defender of the Revolution, both victors and vanquished had to reckon with the genie of nationalism. For some, the easiest way out was to shut their eyes and think only of the pre-1789 past. The relatively enlightened Pius VII returned to the Papal States and promptly abolished street lighting and vaccination.[16] In Turin, the more dimly reactionary

King Victor Emmanuel I arrived back in his city ostentatiously dressed in the fashions of 30 years earlier.

The leading politician of the era was, however, the more complex figure of the Austrian chancellor, Klemens von Metternich. For Metternich, as the young American political scientist Henry Kissinger, in his time to become the 'Metternich of the USA' in the aftermath of its defeat in Vietnam, noted, the burden of government began in the need to 'prop up worm eaten buildings'. Stability at home, Metternich believed, demanded order abroad and vice versa.[17] Freedom, equality and nationalism: each must be opposed.

Metternich, in other words, was a pessimistic conservative, destined to run his course given the inevitability of change, indeed its acceleration as the industrial revolution irresistibly, if erratically, advanced across Europe. Economic growth was expanding cities at a pace unknown in the past. Urbanized life was likely to be harsh, especially for the immigrant workers leaving the peasant world to labour in 'dark, satanic mills' and the other workshops of the world. Faced with macabre evidence of exploitation and death – factors known, too, in the pre-modern city – some of the poor and some of the more enlightened wealthy were becoming preoccupied with the 'social question' and seeking ways to alleviate suffering through national welfare, education, legislation and 'improvement'.

But the cities, in their new suburbs and where planners joined what, throughout the nineteenth century and the first half of the twentieth century, were the swelling ranks of officialdom, were also places that seemed to hurry the march of the rational. New roads were straight; medieval alleys were crooked. Railway lines – the first opened between Darlington and Stockton in

1825 – found the shortest track between one station and the next. Gas lights banished the shadows of night from city streets. With people crammed together and with bureaucrats beginning to investigate and tabulate the human condition, a common vocabulary, a nationalizing language, became mandatory. Statistics began to be collected and the collection often framed nations.[18] Compared with a vast modern factory, even cathedrals began to look small, skew-whiff and irrelevant to human needs in the 'machine age'. At least among those with access to education, religious indifference or anti-clericalism spread.

Ruffled by economic and social change, the political world grew stormy. In 1821, 1830 and then, more drastically in 1848, those who looked back positively on the revolutionary era, who pressed for the revival of liberty and the progress of popular sovereignty, and who believed that the future must belong to them in their merit rather than to purblind priests, degenerate monarchs and their corrupt aristocratic creatures, everywhere organized against the Metternich 'Congress system'. National revolution sprouted anew. Now, it seemed, there might flower a 'springtime of the peoples'. Already in 1835, the Piedmontese younger son of an aristocratic family, Count Camillo Benso di Cavour, expressed his certainty that 'democracy', whether good or bad, was 'the inevitable future of mankind'.[19] In the coming years, humankind could achieve what French 'utopian' socialist, Louis Blanc, memorably sketched as a world where each contributed according to his or her ability and where men and women were protected according to their needs. The era from 1789 to 1815 had not been able to establish the rule of freedom, equality and fraternity, but 1848–49 might be the moment of destiny – first time tragedy, second time victory.

The actual phrase that has echoed through subsequent literature is Marx's: 'the first time as tragedy, the second as farce', a
comment drawn from his reflections in 1852 on the fate of the
Paris revolution, by then converted into the 'Second Empire' of
Napoleon III.[20] The political convulsions that had swept through
every continental European city in 1848–49 had proven evanes-
cent and the reign of *liberté, egalité* and *fraternité* had not come
to pass. As the aristocratic Russian liberal Alexander Herzen,
in exile at Geneva, commented sadly: 'It was not the reaction
that vanquished the revolution. The reaction showed itself
everywhere densely stupid, cowardly, in its dotage . . . [Rather]
the revolution fell, like Agrippina, under the blow of its own
children.'[21] If one revolutionary preferred freedom, another
demanded equality. If one favoured a great Germany, another
sought nationhood for Italians or Poles or Magyars; a 'democratic' member of the Frankfurt Assembly, the parliament of
the German revolution, whose nation-building delegates were
trying to frame the future of Germany and all Central Europe,
confessed that he would 'rather die a thousand times than, for
instance, renounce Trieste because they speak Italian'.[22] In that
port city and gateway to the Adriatic, a century earlier under
reforming Habsburg governance, official recognition had been
granted to the 'nations' of Jews, Greek Orthodox, Armenian
Uniates, Serb Orthodox, Calvinists and Lutherans.[23] But, in
1848, the factors defining community had altered and the city
was transmuted into a potential battleground of the German,
Italian and, potentially, 'Slav' nations, as well as of the Jews who
had long lived there.

If cities were being pummelled into belonging to this or that
nation, what, outside the urban walls (now often being levelled

by the modernizing pickaxe as inefficient medieval leftovers), was to be done with the peasantry, still the majority of Europeans? Marx wrote them off as imponderable and stupid, with one like another as is a potato in a sack of potatoes. In the *Communist Manifesto*, the peasantry was dismissed as a social grouping who were, for all their native willingness to become the hirelings of reaction, destined to disappear with progress, industrialization and the rule of the bourgeoisie.[24] Nor were Marx and Engels alone in their damning of the countryside as barbarous. The Neapolitan sometime revolutionary Vincenzo Cuoco warned that there were 'two, quite separate and antagonistic worlds on the peninsula [of Italy]: one civilised, rational, enlightened and progressive, the other barbaric, ignorant, superstitious and reactionary'.[25] The Frankfurt Assembly, matching practice with thought, tolerated a single peasant among its 831 members and, while it dreamed of ideal constitutions and borders, ignored rural life.[26]

The ruling elites were, capable of discerning that peasant soldiers, usefully not yet nationalized, might help crush urban revolts, and do so the more willingly if they could be instructed that the city dwellers were alien in religion, lifestyle and tongue

The ruling elites were, however, capable of discerning that peasant soldiers, usefully not yet nationalized, might help crush urban revolts, and do so the more willingly if they could be instructed that the city dwellers were alien in religion, lifestyle and tongue. The Austrian Emperor Francis I (1806–35) well understood that he controlled his empire through his ability to move peasant troops from one zone to another:

*My peoples are strange to one another and that is as it should be. They
do not get the same sickness at the same time . . . I send the Hungarians
into Italy, the Italians into Hungary. They do not understand one
another; indeed they hate one another . . . From their antipathy will
be born order and from their mutual hatred general peace.*[27]

National revolution

Nor was the conflict between city and countryside destined to
disappear as the century advanced. Yet, paradoxically, while the
ruthless elite deployment of peasant soldiers threatened freedom, equality and 'progress', 'soil' was becoming one of the
great identifying elements of the nation. As the Italian nationalist composer Giuseppe Verdi made his chorus sing in his opera
I Lombardi (1843), while a warrior band proceeded to a 'holy
land' in Jerusalem but clung all the while to thoughts of their
'Italian' home: '*O monti, o piani, o valli eternamente sacri ad uman
pensier*' (Oh mountains, plains and valleys for ever sacred to
our thought), natural features were more and more hailed as the
determinants of nations. Romanticism had invested nature with
a newly profound and primordial meaning, and it was the Italian
nationalist and revolutionary terrorist Giuseppe Mazzini who
best expressed in his writings and embodied in his life of dedication and self-sacrifice a mystical fusion of men, women and
nature in the nation. So fervent was his message that Mazzini
has been numbered among the wicked progenitors of 'totalitarian democracy' (although a more sympathetic commentator has
portrayed Mazzini instead as a prophet of united Europe, possessed of an essentially 'European mind' and not really a nationalist at all but rather a genuinely democratic anti-communist[28]).

Most historians, however, find that, in regard to the history of nationalism, Mazzini was crucial in his rapturous determination to overthrow the pre-national empires, be they the Habsburgs or the still more ancient Papacy, and replace them with a fresh state system in Europe (the parochial Genoese Mazzini had little interest in the extra-European world, although he did on occasion urge that the 'human race' should be viewed 'without distinction of sex, colour, or condition', with full membership in it 'to be forfeited by crime alone'). Mazzini was equally significant in rejecting the Enlightenment credo that human governance was a rational matter. For Mazzini, it was the soul that mattered. 'The religious spirit', he pronounced, 'never departed from Italy so long as she remained, in spite of her divisions, great and active'. 'The religious sentiment', he added confidently, 'sleeps in our people, waiting to be awakened. He who knows how to rouse it will do more for the nation than can be done by twenty political theories.' Harmonized and blended mystically with God were geography and nature: 'to you, who have been born in Italy, God has allotted, as if favouring you specially, the best-defined country in Europe' (it embraced Istria, Malta, Nice, the Ticino and Corsica, along with what did, after 1860, become Italy). In this extensive programme, it is easy to see why, in the twentieth century, there was a 'Fascist Mazzini' along with the rest. Yet, for this soulful nationalist, the essence of the future and the fount of its religious commitment was indeed the nation: 'Without country you have neither name, token, voice, nor rights, nor admission as brothers into the fellowship of the Peoples. You are bastards of Humanity. Do not beguile yourselves with the hope of emancipation from unjust social conditions if you do not first conquer a country for yourselves.'[29]

Mazzini first penned these words in 1844, but he reworked the article for the publication of his collected works in 1865. By the latter date, quite a bit of conquering had been going on in Europe, some borders had been newly mapped and others soon would be. Italy became a state in 1860–61, Germany in 1870, while, in the restless Balkans, where Ottoman rule had grown feeble, Greece acquired a 'national government' in 1828, Serbia some autonomy in 1816 and, along with Montenegro and Bulgaria, had its independence internationally recognized at the Congress of Berlin in 1878. Romania had been created from a union of the provinces of Moldavia and Wallachia in 1859. In Mazzini's lifetime, Europe was being nationalized as a continental order, with Norway to win its independence in 1905, followed by most of the other present states in 1919 after the First World War.

National counter-revolution

But this territorial and political change occurred in a way that neither the revolutionaries of France nor Mazzini had predicted. In the second half of the nineteenth century, the idea of the nation triumphed, but the practice of certainly equality and perhaps freedom did not. Not revolutionary thinkers but instead two aristocrats, Cavour and Otto von Bismarck, seized the chance to preside over the foundation of Italy and then, a decade later, Germany. Cavour, fond of a bet, a modernizer of his own estates and in touch with liberal luminaries in Paris and London, had begun his role as a nationalizer uncertainly in July 1848 when, in a maiden speech to the Turin Chamber of Deputies, he pronounced: *'S'il y a une vérité incontestable dans le monde, c'est que les Piémontais sont dix fois plus courageux que les Génois'* ('If there is an unchallengeable truth in the world, it is that Piedmontese are ten times braver than Genoese').

Nonetheless, during the next decade, Cavour possessed the acumen and the ruthlessness to become the chief minister of Piedmont and, since that little border state commanded Italy's best army, in that capacity managed the diplomacy and war through which Italy was made in 1859–60. Cavour's tough-minded credo towards the peasants who worked his estates – 'a severe control is the first requisite of good administration'[30] – suggested limits to his liberalism, while his boast *'Je suis italien avant tout'*[31] ('I'm above all an Italian' – French remained his first language) hinted that his own national identity might be infirm. Assisted by a gambler's good luck, however, he was appointed first prime minister of Italy in January 1860 and died in office in June 1861, early enough for most of the equivocations in his life not to harm his historical reputation as a benign 'father of his country', a statesman who oversaw the making of a liberal nation.

Bismarck, by contrast, lived on to be not just the 'maker of modern Germany' but also the chancellor of the German Empire for two decades after 1870. Both his dominant personality and his lengthy career ensure that he is still a focus of debates about an evil German *Sonderweg*, that is, about whether the key role of Germany in fomenting the First and Second World Wars sprang from deep and primary flaws in the nation and were the specific result of the remorseless willingness of German elites to deploy national fervour to divert their populace from demanding greater freedom and more genuine equality.

Certainly imperial and national Germany seemed replete with the triumphs and the contradictions of modernity. The pioneer of the 'second industrial revolution', notably in the chemical and electrical industries, of welfare legislation (it was Bismarck who introduced the national populace to the security of work, health and old-age insurance), of bureaucratic watchfulness and efficiency, of progress towards female equality, of practical education, of organized trade unions, of massive Social Democrat representation in parliament and of a *Weltpolitik* (global foreign policy), Germany, unlike Italy, swiftly became a real great power, potentially the dominant European state. When Kaiser Wilhelm II (reigned 1888–1918) urged that the national policy must always be 'full speed ahead',[32] he seemed to give voice to reality. Yet, as a nation – and much of the rhetoric that hailed economic and social victories was couched in nationalist terms – Germany was founded on an equivocation. A Germany was made but its rule did not extend to all Germans.

During the 1860s, Bismarck, then Prussian chief minister, had erased the old frontiers by winning three wars of aggression, waged against Denmark in 1864, Austria in 1866 and Napoleon III's France in 1870. The battle against Habsburg Austria, which, after its defeat, in 1867 reconstructed itself as Austria-Hungary, had been a conflict among Germans, a dispute over where a German nation might be, whom might belong to it and why a national identity could be restricted or expanded. Bismarck's Prussia was '*kleindeutsch*', not '*grossdeutsch*'. With Bismarck's victories, imperial Germany was to be a nation from which quite a few German-speaking people, from the Habsburg empire and also from imperial Russia and from other ancient settlements in the east, were to be excluded. The pietist Bismarck was anxious for the new Germany to be in majority Protestant and, during the 1870s, reinforced this narrowing by waging a *Kulturkampf* (cultural war) against those Catholics who were beginning to organize politically in his state. These 'enemies within' were cursed in his aggressive vocabulary as *Reichsfeinde* (foes of the Reich), a term that could readily be redirected to flay the fledgling and theoretically internationalist socialist movement. Under Bismarckian impulse, from the first days of their nation state, Germans were thus being trained to see 'othered' sectors of their society who could be blamed for any disaster or apparent disaster. And, as Austria-Hungary, ever more exposed to nationalist resentment against the domination in its administration of German (or Magyar) culture, followed Ottoman Turkey into being the 'sick man of Europe', the possibility lurked that Germany, for all its success, might need to be remade into a polity that ruled all Germans. The circumstances of this nation's birth had it 'encircled' by enemies abroad and at home, before the functioning of the alliance system of pre-1914 Europe sought to curb and control the German state.

A focus on the cunning, toughness and tenacity of such clever and adaptable conservatives as Cavour and Bismarck in perceiving that the lay trinity of the French Revolution could be split asunder and that the appeal of the nation could countermand demands for freedom and equality favours an interpretation of nationalism as an elite invention, little more than a cynical manipulation of tradition. Nor is tradition–invention hard to locate in the two great new nations. Among the Germans' intellectual glories was their primacy in writing and researching history and archaeology, conceived of as rational 'sciences' that displayed national destinies before the political creation of nations. The German mastery of classical studies was given popular and aggressively patriotic representation at the Hermannsdenkmal, a monument to Arminius, opened with ceremony in August 1875. The giant statue of this 'German' victor over the might of the Caesars held a sword proclaiming 'German unity [is] my strength. My strength [is] Germany's power.'[33] The two new nations were not alone in this harnessing of the past. Not only in Italy and Germany but 'in all countries, without exception, archaeologists looked to justify the ethnic, racial, linguistic, religious and/or cultural bases of their nation'.[34]

The Polish model

Yet, although it is clear how drastically nineteenth-century students of the past wrenched it to fit their present desires and opportunities, it would be dishonest not to remark how eerily rapid and fervent a response much nationalist rhetoric won from large strata of the populace. An analyst must ask again whether and why nationalism came from below and what were the effects of the 'genuine popular base' that underpinned *fraternité* more surely than it did other modern ideologies. Poland, unlike Germany and Italy, until 1919 seemingly one of the defeated states of the modern world – the vestiges of its monarchy had been gobbled up in 1796 by its greedy Habsburg, Hohenzollern and Romanov neighbours – offers a neat case study of the problem.

Although the name 'Poland' had been wiped from the map of Europe, its resurrection – nationalists would soon grow accustomed to lauding it as the 'Christ among nations' – remained a possibility throughout the nineteenth century. In 1825, 1830, 1848 and 1863, and then again with the First World War, the existing political settlement endured open challenge. Historian Brian Porter has brilliantly explored this story under the daringly

Although the name 'Poland' had been wiped from the map of Europe, its resurrection – nationalists would soon grow accustomed to lauding it as the 'Christ among nations' – remained a possibility throughout the nineteenth century

confronting title *When Nationalism Began to Hate*.[35] Writing after the so-called 'linguistic turn' and the onset of postmodernity, and anxious to portray national imaginings, Porter, in his account of the development of Polish nationalism, is critical of the softness of the model of a nation as an 'imagined community'. Instead, Porter's story is a sad tracing of the way an optimistic early-nineteenth-century realm, where dissidents envisaged themselves as crusading for 'our freedom and yours', narrowed into a pessimistic, proto-Fascist and anti-Semitic, 'integral', authoritarianism. By 1900, the ambitious nationalist Roman Dmowski was designing a programme wherein 'the only salvation for us is to stop being an incoherent, loose mob, and change into a strongly organized, disciplined army'. 'In relations with other nations', Dmowski added in the deadly social Darwinian terminology taking hold in Europe during those years, 'there is neither right nor wrong, there is only strength and weakness'.[36]

For Porter, this process was one in which 'totalizing narratives of modernization and nationhood' sought to liquidate the previous complexity of the region and to silence the many alternative pre-existing voices. The path to national unity or homogeneity overwhelmed pre-modern heterogeneity. Both elites and the masses bore responsibility for this loss. To some extent, Dmowski and his ilk were driven by the perceived need to 'reconfigure' the nation as 'popular politics' and so serve the people. Yet the nationalist intellectuals made important decisions, thereby conditioning the masses as they surfaced into politics. Ironically, in their self-consciously modern search for science and rationality, for 'coherence and singularity', the radical intellectuals became ever more passionate and desperate, and communicated these emotions to the people. In their blending of past, present and future, the nationalist leaders pushed Polishness down one track of a number that might have been possible. Instead of 'enacting the nation', they increasingly conceived of themselves and the 'people' as embodying it, and so wasted their own chance for free will, even while they extolled liberty. In their noisy assertion of national eternity, they made time run in only one direction and left themselves trapped by its course.

Moreover, another frustration lay ingrained in the processes they favoured since, despite their fervent boasts about achieving unity, the meaning of the nation could only be 'indeterminate, variable and always disputed'. Polishness must always stand under imminent threat. Crusaders who the more they 'won' the more they failed, Polish nationalists, Porter concluded ominously, were certain to opt for hate as soon as there was any halt in national development.[37] Despite the apparent gap in their recent histories, the nation of Poles, like that of the Germans, had as their birthright a deep-seated and ineradicable belief in siege by enemies within and without. The nation's shadowing 'others' were, by definition, cruel and implacable, foes to be instinctively fought, given their profound determination to war against the Poles.

Yet, for the moment no single stream dominated the rest. Until 1919, the peoples of Poland continued to experience the varying rule of Imperial Germany, Russia and Austria-Hungary, while Polish emigrants to Western Europe or the New World had further strands to work into their identity. Still lacking their own nation state, different Poles perforce imagined different communities.

Nationalizing empires

Outside the Americas, vast tracks of the extra-European world were then, either directly or indirectly, being placed under the rule of one or other of the great European powers

In this fate they were scarcely alone. Outside the Americas, vast tracks of the extra-European world were then, either directly or indirectly, being placed under the rule of one or other of the great European powers. Paradoxically, both the 'old nations' of Britain, France, Spain, Portugal and the Netherlands and the new ones of Belgium, Germany and Italy complicated their ethnicity and implicitly infringed the borders of their nations by their zeal to annex 'lesser beings outside the law'. At its birth, nationalism was steeled and contradicted by imperialism. The French were still bloodily beset by the issue during the Algerian crisis of the early 1960s, when the republican theory of equality proved utterly unable to guarantee justice and wellbeing to the Algerian peoples. In the twenty-first century, when debates about immigration and refugees grow more heated, every ex-empire in Europe has not altogether resolved the ethnic complications of their rule and its intrusion into metropolitan histories. A generation earlier, Adolf Hitler, despite his fundamentalist determination to rule Germans only, in practice presided over an imperial state that, with every expansion of its borders, acquired more non-Germans, just as it did whenever it ratcheted up its economy.

Back in the nineteenth century, for the rulers of the European states, Africa, Australasia, much of Asia and, eventually, the Middle East were dismissed as a *terra nullius*, lacking legal base, geography and history until these key features of 'civilization' were imported by imperial administrations. In these 'new worlds', Europeans, loyal to the Enlightenment formula, drew the borders, framed what constitutions there were, catalogued flora and fauna, named rivers, mountains, towns and roads, and invented identities for whole peoples. Proud as the bearers of that 'progress' and 'science' resulting from the successive industrial and technological revolutions, the Europeans begged no pardons in their feelings of superiority, their 'Orientalism' writ large. European cultural imperialism in the second half of the nineteenth century was still less repentant than had been that of the Napoleonic armies invading the Italian peninsula. The colonizers occupied the world, with its existing unruliness, untidiness and variety, thinking

The colonizers occupied the world, with its existing unruliness, untidiness and variety, thinking as 'enlightened' Europeans, expecting the subject peoples to 'catch up' and be quick about it

as 'enlightened' Europeans, expecting the subject peoples to 'catch up' and be quick about it. 'Terrible simplifiers' have afflicted many sectors of the histories of humankind in the modern era, but imperialism is always an activity where their arrogance, insouciance and determination flourish.

Imperialized empires

More than a century later, it is only too evident that the 'white' invasions of the nineteenth century collided with complex and delicate existing societal systems. The resulting smash was especially great in China, Japan, Korea, Vietnam, India, Ethiopia and Persia, each an empire of antiquity and breadth. What were the results for the idea and the practice of the nation on the peoples into whose histories Europe had irrupted?

Nowadays, the victories of the nation have ensured that historians of the Chinese, Japanese, Korean, Vietnamese, Indian, Ethiopian and Iranian 'nation states' maintain that a national resistance of greater or lesser weight blocked or diverted European intrusion. The new nations of the developing world in the era of decolonization after 1945, ironically reflecting what the reconstituted or new nations of Europe had done in the past, have each sought to frame an eternal history that maximized its territory and human significance.

A classic African example appears in Zimbabwe, where, it is averred, ruins at 'Great Zimbabwe' prove the existence of a medieval Shona state in the same way that other ruins or memories of battle had, by 1870, justified the claims to nationhood of Serbs, Italians and Germans. The initial flutterings of a search for national freedom in the colonial world inevitably cast in thought patterns imported from Europe and based on 'more aggressive and exclusive understandings of nationality' than had been the norm in the older empires, can already be discerned in the late nineteenth century. So, too, can another phenomenon of our own times and one that will preoccupy this analysis in a later chapter. In 1893, the seer Swami Vivekansada, attending the World Parliament of Religion in Chicago, meshed Hinduism and the 'Indian nation'. In the extra-European world, God was not dead; despite the Enlightenment, religions grew everywhere during the nineteenth century and simultaneously hardened their beliefs, giving lip service to contemporary cultural change by making their credo ostensibly more rational and scientific.[38] In Persia, as it was still generally called around the same time, another exclusionary feature of early nationalist discourse was a tightening of gender roles. The nationalist Mirza Malkom Khan and his journal *Qanun* (The Law) berated the weak Qajar regime for emasculating Iranian men. He and his friends envisaged a more manly national future when a united people would prevent the continued 'rape' of the country by foreigners.[39] In many societies, means were being found to marry ancient beliefs, rendered more viciously exclusive by modern preoccupations about accurate categorization, and new ideas about national identity.

Racialized nations

While Europe still ruled the waves, there was another disturbing corollary of viewing the world as a grouping of peoples. When observed closely, the definition of the domestic national base of the old and new European empires was not necessarily simple. What part did the Catalans and Basques play in Spain, the Irish, Welsh, Scots (and English) in 'Great Britain', the peoples of all the Russias in the Romanov empire? Even in new Italy and new Germany, there were minorities reluctant to own to being Italians or Germans. In further irony, what did it mean for national homogeneity when Europeans ruled outside Europe? What part were colonial peoples to be given in the nation? The main response to this question was 'very little'. The extra-European subjects of the empires, when and if educated, might share a language, a religion, a loyalty to a monarch or to the institutions of a Republic, even habits, cuisine and a 'culture', the wares of the missionaries of a Christian god and of the nation, with the folks back home. But rarely were they acknowledged to be the equals of the metropolitan power or able to aspire to full assimilation into the nation.

Why was this so, especially when colonialism brought at least some intermarriage as well as alteration to the original metropolitan understanding of life and the world caused by colonial factors? The answer would prove deadly. If the nation was fusing them at home, 'race' was ensuring that the European global superiority over subject peoples was permanent and predetermined. But what was a race, and how could it be measured?

No definitive answer can be given to this question, all the more because race and nation became terms that were, and remain, on occasion, exchangeable in almost every state setting. Until 1945, and even beyond, race could seem the more objective term, a matter that could be measured scientifically through cranial shape, bloodstocks or gene pools. But racial theoreticians found it difficult not to move from their statistics to philosophy and metaphysics, and regularly maintained that the statistical detail must mean something more, especially something 'spiritual'. Here a key figure was Arthur de Gobineau (1816–82). This reactionary French bourgeois shored up his own doubtful social status and gave impetus to his rejection of the French Revolution by publishing, in 1853–55, his lengthy and meandering 'Essay on the inequality of the human races'. History lay at its centre. De Gobineau began with the 'fall of civilizations', an event, he argued, that was always occasioned by racial contamination. Degeneration came because a people 'has no longer the same blood in its veins, continual adulterations having gradually affected the quality of that blood'.[40] De Gobineau never managed to come in from the cold politically, but France remained a society scarred by racist assumptions, with the anti-Semitic side of the issue being given special play in the Dreyfus case that preoccupied the political world for much of the 1890s and the following decade.

Russia, Britain, Italy, the USA – each society similarly heard debates about race and its impact on the nation. During the belle époque, every European society worried about its possible degeneration and looked to mass sport, mass conscription, the greater availability of medical welfare and a more rigorously applied nationalism to ensure that its own nation was to be a winner and not among the vanquished in the great struggle of the peoples for existence. Only then could the nation be readied for the war that, it was widely assumed among the 'generation of 1914', must soon 'test' the competing nations. Socialists and capitalists, in their competing ways, may have still talked as though the nation and race were not the future, which was instead to be necessarily global. Pacifists, organizing as never before, may have dreamed of a world without war. But the followers of these ideas, too, felt the tug of the moment and were rarely oblivious to their nations. One example was the Italian pacifist E.T. Moneta, winner of the Nobel Peace Prize in 1907, who nonetheless contended, when Italy violently seized the Turkish territories of Tripolitania and Cyrenaica in 1911, that the aggression was justified to save his nation from being enclosed by an 'iron-ring' in the Mediterranean.[41]

The national and racial unconscious

The eventual Nazi Judaeocide, however, has made imperial Germany and Austria-Hungary the most notorious sites of pre-1914 racist theory and of the surfacing of political movements placing race at the centre of their appeal and motivation. One nondescript lower-middle-class young man in pre-1914 Vienna was Adolf Hitler. As he remembered in *Mein Kampf*, when he moved in from the provinces, 'I was repelled by the conglomeration of races which the capital showed me, repelled by the whole mixture of Czechs, Poles, Hungarians, Ruthenians, Serbs, and Croats, and everywhere, the eternal mushroom of humanity – Jews and more Jews.'[42] Hitler's political hero became the Christian Social local mayor, Karl Lueger, a ruthlessly cynical politician who fostered and cashed in on popular anti-Semitism; Hitler recalled him as having carried on his coat-tails 36 anti-Semitic members to the city council and as being 'the greatest German of all times'.[43] For Hitler, race, nation and an unrelenting battle against what he saw as the cosmopolitan evils of Jewry and, after 1917, of 'Bolshevism' warmed his fundamentalism to boiling point.

Yet the better embodiment of all that was perplexing about the approach of modernity and the accompanying spread of national identity in the twentieth century was another citizen of the Habsburg state, a generation older than Hitler. Sigmund Freud (1856–1939) was born to a middle-class Jewish family in Freiburg in Moravia, a city of Germanic culture and language in the Czech lands of the empire. A precocious child, young Sigmund was told when 11 years old that he would naturally rise to be a government minister.[44] Freud himself would later recall dreaming of leading the conquest of Rome as a new Hannibal, although self-analysis eventually intimated that he was actually thinking about how 'the German language might be better tolerated in Prague' and worrying over 'the Jewish problem, [with its] concern about the future of one's children to whom one cannot give a country of their own, concern about educating them in such a way that they can move freely across frontiers'.[45]

Hans Kohn

Between the wars and then after 1945, one of the most important and influential historians of nations and nationalism was Hans Kohn. His book *The Idea of Nationalism: A Study of its Origins and Background* (1944, London: Macmillan) can be read as a summary of the liberal democratic world's understanding of the subject as the Allies moved to victory over Nazi-fascism.

Kohn was born in Prague in 1891 to a German-speaking Jewish family and lived in the eventual capital of the Czechoslovak (after 1990, just Czech) nation state. As he phrased it in his autobiography 'the very air of Prague made me a student of history and of nationalism'. When the spirit of the times darkened, Kohn, who had travelled between Paris, London and Jerusalem, first abandoned the Zionist movement, dismayed by the violent dispute that had broken out with Palestinian Arabs in 1929, and then, in 1934, joined the intellectual diaspora to the USA, where he made a new life and a successful academic career.

Kohn was not fully convinced about the novelty of the nation. The national idea, he argued, had a long history. Classical Greeks and pre-Christian Jews clung to a 'group-sentiment of tribalism' that separated them from other people and offered a rich inheritance: 'This consciousness, shared by every individual, raised him [sic] to a new personal dignity, and prepared the spiritual foundations of democracy.' Yet, Kohn also knew that there was much that was evil in the world of nations in which he lived. Nationalism, he reiterated, was 'first and foremost a state of mind, an act of consciousness', while also being 'modern' in the sense that it began to matter only once the masses were experiencing it.

How, he wondered, could the happy politics and society he found in the Anglo-Saxon world, its pleasing and fruitful harnessing of liberty, welfare and nationality, have become so threatened by the terrible racism of the Nazis? The answer was simple. In modern times, nationalism was two-faced. Our era was one of battle between the rival forms of nationalism. In western Europe and North America, a liberal view of the nation had begun to take hold during the Enlightenment. It aimed 'to limit government power and to secure civil rights'.

This good nationalism was, however, shadowed by a bad. In Germany and further east, Kohn argued, from the moment of the failure of the 1848 revolutions, darker principles took root. A love of native land was corrupted by violence and government power, and so eventually by 'totalitarianism'. Moreover, in the wider world, Arab nationalism in the Middle East, but not the Jewish patriotism favoured by those mooting the state of Israel, nor the 'modernized' nationalism of Kemal Atatürk in post-1919 Turkey, threatened mayhem. There might even be problems in Zionism, in regard to which Kohn, late in his life, reiterated his fear that it was going 'the way of most Central and Eastern European nationalisms'.

Kohn's division, despite its crudity, was destined to become a central assumption in many analyses of the subject and has still not disappeared from the literature.

Freud was to have many reasons to regret the politics of the nation. When he was still a toddler, his merchant father moved first to Leipzig and then, in 1860, to Vienna to escape Czech hostility, the Jewish family rendered uneasy by the initial expression of a local sense of nationality. The year of their arrival in the Habsburg capital was itself ironical, given that it was then that Italy became a nation state, with the Freud family allegedly remarking that young Sigmund resembled Giuseppe Garibaldi, the peerless 'Hero of Two Worlds' and conqueror of the south for the new Italy. For a time, the teenage Freud dreamed of a law degree, the classic preparation for administration and politics. In Vienna, however, enveloping anti-Semitism was restricting entry for Jews to such courses and, instead, Freud trained in medicine, while rejecting occasional thoughts of emigration to 'America, Australia or anywhere else', a choice that would have entailed drastic alteration in his national identity.[46]

Thereafter, Freud, with much travail, pursued a brilliant career in that *fin-de-siècle* Vienna, governed by Lueger, that was grappling with Austro-Marxism, German nationalism and political anti-Semitism,[47] as well as with the more immediate dilemma of how the institutions of the Habsburg dynasty could cope with the swelling surge of the nations. In 1914, the issue of the Austro-Hungarian Empire's right to rule non-Germans in the Balkans sparked the First World War. Learning of the outbreak of open conflict, Freud, perhaps still half hoping to be a Habsburg Hannibal, was excited: 'All my libido is given to Austria-Hungary', he expostulated.[48]

The issue of the national identity of the Freuds deserves analysis. Freud's family were middle class, natural liberals. The fact that they were also of Jewish religion and culture made them followers of an ideology that had freed them from the ghetto and opened

Freud's family were middle class, natural liberals. The fact that they were also of Jewish religion and culture made them followers of an ideology that had freed them from the ghetto and opened opportunity to the individual to make life his own

opportunity to the individual (like those new Hannibals, Napoleon and Garibaldi) to make life his own. But, from 1848, with every passing year, the relationship between liberty and nationality became more tormenting. Should Freud opt therefore to be a German (liberal) nationalist? Much suggested that he should. Yet, Bismarck and Prussia had seized German nationality as their own. From 1870, the destiny of Austria was either to be, as actually happened in the First World War, a patronized and inferior 'noble second' or to collapse into its national composite parts. Many Austrian Germans, who sensed where history was going, were converted to German nationalism, with Georg von Schönerer of Freud's generation being most notorious. When Freud mooted unleashing his unconscious passions, his *libido* or *id*, behind the Habsburg forces in 1914, he was deluding himself. The power of the nation blunted any leftover thrust in multinational or dynastic ideas. And Freud's own life story was heading towards the trauma of the war and its destruction of a Habsburg future, the rise of the Nazis and the Judaeocide, the *Anschluss* of March 1938 and the psychoanalyst's flight to exile and death in London.

Somewhere in the shadows, a rival course being mapped in pre-1914 Vienna, that site of so many of the stresses and traumas of modernity, was that to be credited to Theodor Herzl, the prophet of Zionism. As a philosopher, Herzl clung to many liberal ideals. How absurd, he argued, to opt for Hebrew as the language of a

Herzl clung to many liberal ideals. How absurd, he argued, to opt for Hebrew as the language of a Jewish state: 'After all, we can't speak Hebrew with each other

Jewish state: 'After all, we can't speak Hebrew with each other. Who among us knows enough to ask for a railway ticket in that language?'[49] Perhaps a restored Zion could be a place of many tongues, he mused, and, logically, German might provide its unifying language (and culture). The Freuds might have found a contented identity in such a sophisticated and enlightened Jewish state. Failing its arrival, it might be thought that Sigmund Freud invented (traumatic) sex because, in his special circumstance, cut off from the pleasures of a non-Jewish and non-Habsburg European bourgeois, he could not wring emotional satisfaction from the nation. Sigmund Freud could not make harmonious the trinity of liberty, equality and fraternity and was left instead to devote his life scientifically to detecting and describing human irrationality and the unconscious. In Freud's vision, Enlightenment rationality was not enough to comprehend or drive the world.

Notes

1 R. Gildea, *The Past in French History* (1994, New Haven, CT: Yale University Press), p. 15.

2 D.A. Bell, 'Lingua popoli, lingua dei: language, religion, and the origins of French revolutionary nationalism', *American Historical Review*, 1995, 100, pp. 1219, 1227.

3 M. Wollstonecraft, *A Vindication of the Rights of Women* (ed. C.W. Hagelman) (1967, New York: Norton).

4 O. Hufton, 'Women in revolution 1789–1796', *Past and Present*, 1971, 53, p. 107.

5 *Ibid.* p. 108.

6 L. Gershoy, *The Era of the French Revolution, 1789–1799: Ten Years that Shook the World* (1957, Princeton, NJ: Van Nostrand), p. 129.

7   E. Wilson, *To the Finland Station: A Study in the Writing and Acting of History* (1960, London: Fontana) p. 30.

8   M. Broers, *The Napoleonic Empire in Italy, 1796–1814: Cultural Imperialism in a European Context?* (2005, Houndmills: Palgrave), pp. 1–2, 33.

9   *Ibid.* p. 68.

10   J.K. Moorhead (ed.), *Conversations of Goethe with Eckermann* (1930, London: Dent) pp. 245–6.

11   I. Woloch, 'Napoleonic conscription: state power and civil society', *Past and Present*, 1986, 111, p. 101.

12   L. Bergeron, *France under Napoleon* (1981, Princeton, NJ: Princeton University Press), pp. xiii–xiv.

13   R. Cobb, *The Police and the People: French Popular Protest 1789–1820* (1972, London: Oxford University Press), p. 197.

14   J.G. von Herder, *Reflections on the Philosophy of the History of Mankind* (ed. F.E. Manuel) (1968, Chicago, IL: University of Chicago Press), pp. 58, 61, 98, 112.

15   S.J. Woolf (ed.), *Nationalism in Europe, 1815 to the Present: A Reader* (1996, London: Routledge), p. 9.

16   S.J. Woolf, *A History of Italy 1700–1860: The Social Constraints of Political Change* (1979, London: Methuen), p. 243.

17   H. Kissinger, *A World Restored* (1964, New York: Grosset and Dunlap).

18   For a case study, see S. Patriarca, *Numbers and Nationhood: Writing Statistics in Nineteenth-Century Italy* (1996, Cambridge: Cambridge University Press).

19   J.A. Davis, *Conflict and Control: Law and Order in Nineteenth Century Italy* (1988, London: Macmillan), p. 146.

20   K. Marx, 'The eighteenth Brumaire of Louis Bonaparte' in *Surveys from Exile* (ed. D. Fernbach) (1973, Harmondsworth: Penguin), p. 146.

21 A. Herzen, *My Past and Thoughts*, vol. II (1968, London: Chatto and Windus), p. 741.

22 L.B. Namier, *Vanished Supremacies* (1958, Harmondsworth: Penguin), p. 65.

23 L.C. Dubin, *The Port Jews of Habsburg Trieste: Absolutist Politics and Enlightenment Culture* (1999, Stanford, CA: Stanford University Press), p. 14.

24 K. Marx and F. Engels, *The Communist Manifesto* (ed. A.J.P. Taylor) (1967, Harmondsworth: Penguin), p. 91.

25 Davis, *Conflict and Control*, p. 120.

26 V. Valentin, *1848: Chapters of German History* (1940, London: George Allen and Unwin), p. 271. There were no 'workers'.

27 A. Milne, *Metternich* (1975, London: University of London Press), p. 119.

28 J. Talmon, *The Myth of the Nation and the Vision of Revolution: The Origins of Ideological Polarisation in the Twentieth Century* (1980, London: Secker and Warburg), p. 7; D. Mack Smith, *Mazzini* (1994, New Haven, CT: Yale University Press), pp. 12, 52, 221.

29 J. Mazzini, *The Duties of Man and Other Essays* (1907, London: Dent), pp. 30–31, 53, 240.

30 R. Romeo, *Cavour e il suo tempo (1842–1854)*, vol. I (1977, Bari: Laterza), pp. 133, 333.

31 E.M. Cesaresco, *Cavour* (1898, London: Macmillan), p. v.

32 M. Kitchen, *The Silent Dictatorship: The Politics of the German High Command under Hinderburg and Ludendorff, 1916–1918* (1976, London: Croom Helm), p. 17.

33 I. Wiwjorra, 'German archaeology and its relation to nationalism and racism', in M. Diaz-Andrieu and T. Champion (eds), *Nationalism and Archaeology in Europe* (1996, London: UCL Press), p. 92.

34 M. Diaz and T. Champion, 'Nationalism and archaeology in Europe: an introduction', in Diaz-Andrieu and Champion, *Nationalism and Archaeology in Europe*, p. 11.

35 B. Porter, *When Nationalism Began to Hate: Imagining Modern Politics in Nineteenth-Century Poland* (2000, New York: Oxford University Press).

36 *Ibid.* pp. 10, 155.

37 *Ibid.* pp. 5–6, 14, 16, 59, 136, 145, 177.

38 C.A. Bayly, *The Birth of the Modern World 1780–1914: Global Connections and Comparisons* (2004, Oxford: Blackwell), pp. 218, 222, 341–2.

39 J. De Groot, 'The dialectics of gender: women, men and political discourse in Iran c. 1890–1930', *Gender and History*, 1993, 5, pp. 261–2.

40 A. De Gobineau, *Selected political writings* (ed. M. Biddiss) (1970, London: Jonathan Cape), p. 59.

41 R.J.B. Bosworth, *Italy and the Approach of the First World War* (1983, London: Routledge), p. 72.

42 A. Hitler, *Mein Kampf* (ed. D.C. Watt) (1969, London: Hutchinson), p. 113.

43 *Ibid.* p. 51; A. Hitler, *Table Talk 1941–4* (ed. H. Trevor-Roper) (1953, London: Weidenfeld and Nicolson), p. 147.

44 E. Jones, *The Life and Work of Sigmund Freud* (ed. L. Trilling and S. Markus) (1964, Harmondsworth: Penguin), p. 34.

45 S. Freud, *The Interpretation of Dreams* (ed. J. Strachey, A. Tyson and A. Richards) (1991, Harmondsworth: Penguin), pp. 282–4, 573.

46 Jones, *The Life and Work of Sigmund Freud*, pp. 34, 171. Among other escape routes used and then abandoned was cocaine (p. 104). See also W.J. McGrath, *Freud's Discovery of Psychoanalysis: The Politics of Hysteria* (1986, Ithaca, NY: Cornell University Press), pp. 95–7.

47 For a brilliant portrait, see C.E. Schorske, *Fin-de-siècle Vienna: Politics and Culture* (1980, New York: Knopf).

48 Jones, *The Life and Work of Sigmund Freud*, pp. 424, 426, 483.

49 Quoted by Schorske, *Fin-de-siècle Vienna*, p. 172.

CHAPTER 4

Imperial, national, racial and world war, 1914–45

THE FIRST HALF OF THE TWENTIETH CENTURY is still notorious as the time of unparalleled human suffering and death. The First World War, revolution and civil war in Russia, Fascism, Nazism and the Depression, Japanese assaults both on imperial powers and on their Asian neighbours – the list of disasters is long and familiar. Between 1914 and 1945, perhaps 150 million people died 'prematurely' for political and ideological reasons. Although national pieties have worked to conceal the matter, this second and still more devastating '30-years war' was in many ways the result of the world's drift into an ever more steely determination to be divided into nations, just as each war, and each crisis, made each national cause seem to the great majority of the world's peoples the more just and virtuous. In these 'locust years', the deadly nationalization of human empathy advanced everywhere and no matter what the cost.

The First World War and the Serb people

The First World War began the process. Its track is framed by two dates. On 28 June 1914, the tubercular poet and Serb nationalist Gavrilo Princip assassinated Archduke Franz Ferdinand, the Habsburg heir to the throne of Austria-Hungary, and his morganatic wife while they were on an official visit to Sarajevo, capital of the recently annexed province of Bosnia. On 28 June 1919, the delegates of the defeated German nation, in the process at home of becoming a liberal democratic republic, signed at Versailles outside Paris the treaty that ended the First World War (and, in its contradictions, it was later frequently maintained, inexorably led to the second conflict).

This list is incomplete. A third date fluttered somewhere in the ether in 1914 and resurfaced when Wilsonian self-determination triumphed in 1919. On 28 June 1389, at 'Blackbirds' field' in Kosovo, the forces of the medieval Serb empire were over-whelmed by the greater power of the Ottoman Empire, a loss that signalled the collapse of a 'Serb state' for almost 500 years. The clash was destined not to be forgotten. Instead it was inscribed into the national myth of the Serbs and, certainly from the nineteenth century, became a key element of Serb identity. In 1877–78, during the crisis of Ottoman rule that was settled diplomatically at the Congress of Berlin with the recognition of full national sovereignty for the Balkan states, there were already drastic examples of 'ethnic cleansing', as it would come to be known, in the territory surrounding the town of Pristina, the capital of Kosovo. During the Balkan wars of 1912–13, the ex-pulsions and massacres in the region grew worse, claiming tens of thousands of victims and being by no means restricted to

Serbs and Muslim Kosovars. The deaths did not cease in the Great War. Nor did the Second World War avoid the welter of blood. In the circumstances, it is not altogether surprising that the lost medieval battle is still evoked in that present-day Serbia that teeters on the edge of being a 'rogue state', while the semi-autonomous territory of Kosovo remains disputed between Serbs and Kosovars and is necessarily patrolled for the foreseeable future by United Nations forces.

The First World War

When the First World War is understood as a grandiose struggle of the nations, then, in this corner of Europe, the earth still shudders from the national hatred enacted at that time. It is a complication that, outside the Balkans, the great conflict was fought not so much between nation states but between empires, still governed by ancient dynasties: on the one side the Habsburg and Hohenzollern empires, joined from October 1914 by their imperial Ottoman clients; on the other the Romanov Russian and Saxe-Coburg-Gotha or Windsor British empires (and Savoyard Italians), bolstered by a national French Republic. But France, despite being the child of the revolution of 1789, had since 1815 become a global empire.

Maoris, Fijians, Vietnamese, Senegalese, Chechens, Georgians, Somalis, Eritreans and many others had to count their war dead, an oblation at imperial command. Nonetheless, in every country,

The First World War was marketed to the soldiery and home population as a conflict of the nations or as a divine test of national power and devotion

the First World War was marketed to the soldiery and home population as a conflict of the nations or as a divine test of national power and devotion. One of the fundamental effects of war propaganda was a popular nationalization of empathy and sympathy. A struggle that was so massive and that counted deaths in the millions had to find some explanation that was greater than the naked moment of individual 'sacrifice'. The dead had to have offered themselves for the collective.

In practice, soldiers often fought, killed and died for their 'mates', for that small group among whom they were living and to whom they were presently bonded in the extraordinary circumstances, the all but troglodyte conditions, of the trenches. Yet the confined nature of much comradeship was not destined to be 'remembered with advantages', as Shakespeare had understood those recalling war. Rather than the platoon or company, it was the nation that was destined to command memory of the front. Soldiers and their families on the one hand, and generals and politicians on the other, found the morale to continue, both in war and, after 1918, in peace, in the idea of a seamless connection between present, past and future and so of a national eternity. The appalling death toll of the war, and the lasting physical and psychological maiming of so many combatants that was the necessary result of the tactics and technology of the period, could best be justified by the view that the immediate sacrifice made sense in the timelessness of the nation and in the godly justice of its cause. As cenotaphs and tombs to unknown soldiers were inaugurated in the various combatant states once peace was secured, these most national of monuments preached, more openly than had been true before 1914, the gospel of the religion of the nation. They literally made concrete the popular span and the exclusivity of national belonging – war memorials solemnly listed the war dead of each nation and from all social groups in it but did nothing to record or honour those whom the avowedly pure, crusading warriors of the nation had killed, crippled or raped.

The war was having other deleterious effects on those who fought it. The length of combat and its geographical spread, and the way most fronts bogged down for months or years, enhanced the demand for total commitment. Nationalized war was too serious a matter to be left to the professionals. In every country, means were sought to maximize the efficiency of factories and farms, to unite the population, by force if need be, so they could work night and day for the war effort. Above all, measures were enacted to bond the conscripted soldiers and the home front as never before. The war was cultural or it was nothing. Gender, class, age, region, religion, heritage, individuality – each sphere where distinctions actually existed now had to deny variation and cleave to the nation. Opposition, doubt, criticism and difference were scarcely to be tolerated in even the most liberal combatant states. Waging a total war could only be an absolute activity, where any infringing of national unity must be read as treason or worse.

Nonetheless, for all the hailing of the war, its theory and practice were not the same. Russia and Italy can provide examples of the authoritarian and the liberal hope for adamantine social unity and of the fickle practical limits of nationalization through and for war.

The First World War and all the Russias

Before 1914, Romanov Russia displayed its backwardness in the hesitancy with which it summoned nationalism to shore up the dynasty's rule. The result of this lack of political modernity was, by 1917, civil and military collapse – 'revolution'. Imperial Russia failed the 'test of war'. It was true that, in 1913, the tercentenary of Romanov rule, there had been some experiment with a vocabulary of Russian nationalism. A historian could urge that the accession of Tsar Michael, after the devastating time of troubles when the Poles had reached Moscow, signified, in 1613, the birth of the nation. In an unprecedented manner for Russia, a life of Nicholas II declared that the present Tsar was proud of a Russian identity, evident in his fondness for borscht and bliny and his preference for Russian champagne as a tipple.

Given that Russians (and defining them was by no means a simple matter) composed only about half of Nicholas's subjects, such nationalizing could not proceed too far, however, and there was always an accompanying thought that what modernity really entailed was 'popular autocracy', a situation where 'the Russian people were very clearly aware that it was as impossible to live without a Tsar as it was to live without a head'.[1] Tsarist Russia was not a society where evocations of popular sovereignty and democratic citizenship could become too wide-ranging.

Although, in 1914, this Russia entered the war riding a wave of patriotism occasioned by battle against what could be portrayed as traditional Germanic foes, any mass enthusiasm was soon dissipated and Romanov Russia demonstrated that it had not yet been forged into an imagined community. 'Patriotic imagery reveals that Russians had a pretty clear idea against whom they were fighting in the war, but not for whom and for what.'[2]

Something more perilous soon became evident about the effort of this not fully nationalized society as it conducted a war of greater momentum than was proving possible on the Western

Front. The conflict provided a 'social and temporal space of "violent migrations" . . . Some of the people located in this space perpetrated violence, others suffered it, and very many did both, but all were living with a radically new social and political ecosystem that shaped their behavior in important ways.'[3] The rapid and broad movement of the front thrust war, rapidly perceived as both external and internal, directly into the lives of many people and did so with toxic effects both for those at the top of society and those at the bottom. Identifying allegedly ubiquitous spies and saboteurs and 'cleansing' corrupt areas of threatening groups became an every day event. Jews were especially likely to be victimized, with a million subject to forced deportation, but the realm where everyone, including the soldiers, was either a migrant or a refugee was fundamentally 'desocialized'. In the new bleakness, there may have been a search to imagine community but the greater effect was the pervasive certainty that menacing 'others' stalked the land whose frightful purpose could be deflected only by their deportation or death.

> *The realm where everyone, including the soldiers, was either a migrant or a refugee was fundamentally 'desocialized'*

Wartime identity in many of the Russias may have been unreliably nationalized, but the conflict was teaching the subjects of the Russian empire how to hate in a national manner.

The First World War and the Italian nation

The story of the Italian version of the First World War has some parallels with the Russian. 'Liberal' Italy, the least of the great powers, entered the struggle late and fought its own Alpine and hill campaigns against Austro-Hungarian armies over disputed territory that ran from the Trentino/Alto Adige to the Adriatic. In October–November 1917, Italy, routed by combined Austro-German forces at Caporetto, almost followed Russia out of the war and into socialist revolution. Its forces were, however, stiffened by French and British support and the armies of the central powers ran out of steam just short of Venice and the gateway to the Po plain. Italy thus passed its test of war and, in 1918, celebrated national victory. Yet, the idiosyncratic war that Italian society waged led directly to xenophobic fascism and aggressively nationalist dictatorship; Benito Mussolini became prime minister in October 1922 and instituted open tyranny in January 1925.[4]

The favourite word by which this regime was to describe itself was 'totalitarian'. It is easy to trace the origins of what has been called the 'totalitarian seduction' to Italy's war. The presence of lingering queries over the profundity of Italy's liberal institutions and of the success of the nationalization of a populace, who did not reliably speak a single national language, and clung to regional, local and familial cultures and patterns of behaviour, gave one cause for anxiety. A more specific problem was created through the lack of a *union sacrée*, given Italy's belated and politically manipulated war entry; most Italian socialists and many Catholics remained at best lukewarm to crusading for the nation.

As a result, nationalist talk became the more stentorian and unforgiving. Already in 1914, Alfredo Rocco, the nationalist and later fascist minister of justice and architect of the legislative basis of the totalitarian state, laid claim to the ownership of time in a new way and, in so doing, highlighted what would prove the limits of Italian liberalism. 'The individual', Rocco wrote, 'is a transient and infinitesimal part of the nation . . . The nation must never be sacrificed to the individual. Rather, when need be, the individual should be sacrificed to the nation.'[5]

After Italy entered the conflict, the urgent desire among patriots to overcome Italian backwardness and engage in total war as a modern and united people increased. Even though European 'scientific' racists had assigned Italians a lowly rank in the hierarchy of racial virtue and Italy's most internationally celebrated intellectual, the (Jewish) criminologist Cesare Lombroso, had based his own theory on a primordial difference between those who lived in the north of the peninsula and southerners, talk about blood became common. The vice of the enemy Germans, it was now maintained, had deep historical roots. Somewhat confusingly, they embodied eternal barbarity, uncomprehending of the light and civilization of Rome, and were simultaneously the germ-laden carriers of an inhumanly industrialized society, the evil face of modernity.[6] Just like the Russians, Italians, who defined themselves through the nation, now feared enemies within – spies, 'socialists', foreigners, potentially Jews. All could hide and work their evil will because of the presence in Italian society of rootlessness, heterogeneity, confusion and complexity, national disunity.

> *Just like the Russians, Italians, who defined themselves through the nation, now feared enemies within – spies, 'socialists', foreigners, potentially Jews*

As a result, the more pessimistic Italian nationalists concluded that violence and the subordination of the individual to the national community were necessary to Italy's future existence.

Their commitment to the retention of liberal institutions in Italy was shallow, as events would soon prove. After 1922, the practice of fascism would itself scarcely opt for simplicity or for a neat relationship between theory and practice. Yet few Italian nationalists saw much to lament in the dictatorship during its rule for a generation after 1922. When the defence of the nation was evoked, Italian liberalism was, for the greatest part, only a fair weather friend of freedom.

Woodrow Wilson and a liberal, capitalist and national peace

Despite the turmoil in Russia and Italy, when battle ceased it still seemed probable that, in Europe and in the rest of the globe, the causes proclaimed in the Enlightenment had taken another step forward through the French and Anglo-Saxon, 'western' victory in the war said to have been waged to end war. The great symbol of a just and fair peace was the Democrat president of the USA, Woodrow Wilson, a man who had trained himself for politics by a career in academic social science and history-writing.[7] It was Wilson who urged that the post-war world would marry anew *liberté* and *fraternité*, freedom and the nation, in a world-ranging organization and through the doctrine of 'self-determination'. As he advised his counsellors, with studied innocence, when setting out for the Old World: 'Tell me what's right and I'll fight for it.'[8] In 'a new order', all the nations, he proclaimed, must consecrate themselves to real brotherhood.[9]

After the president and his team reached Paris, the peacemakers expended much energy in sketching exact borders for such 'new' states as Czechoslovakia, Latvia, Lithuania, Estonia, Poland and

Yugoslavia and for such redesigned ones as Germany, Austria, Hungary, Italy, Belgium and France. The sordidly self-interested secret treaties of the 'old diplomacy' must be set aside, Wilson vowed. A new age of 'open agreements openly arrived at' must eliminate lingering conflict through international law and government. A League of Nations must adjust national disputes through just arbitration.

Alas for these hopes and prophecies. It was not long before the young economist J.M. Keynes, who attended the peacemaking as an expert, was bitingly dismissing the US president as a 'blind and deaf Don Quixote'.[10] The last months of Wilson's presidency brought political disaster and an overwhelming defeat for the Democrat Party in November 1920, with the victory of the isolationist Republican Warren Harding. The USA did not join the League of Nations and, for all its achievements in the social arena, the body based in Geneva proffered a frail defence against the many national disputes of the inter-war world. Ever since, commentators have wondered whether the problem was Wilson's global 'idealism' or his only half-concealed fondness for personal advantage and national American self-interest. This southern Democrat was no enthusiast for Mexican revolution or for the admission of Japan as a genuine great power in the Pacific and also disdained black equality and trade union freedom within the USA.

Wilson versus Lenin

Yet, in regard to the history of nationalism, the greater trouble with the post-war peacemaking brewed elsewhere. One issue lay in the east, in the implicit conflict between the recipe offered by the liberal capitalist USA and its friends and that being purveyed by the infant Bolshevik state, still struggling to hold on to the rule of the Russias and engaged in a brutal and bloody civil war. As American left Democrat Arno Mayer, locating origins for the post-1945 Cold War in the period following the First World War, maintained, maybe Versailles was really a conflict between the Wilsonian marriage of liberalism and nationalism and the Leninist mixture of authoritarian communism and internationalism.[11]

Whatever may be thought of Mayer's backdating of the Cold War, he was right to see Wilson as repackaging for the old continent a formula that had been experimented with in Europe during the 1848 revolutions and then found wanting. Certainly the application of the Wilson model soon proved unhappy as the First World War led to the Second and inter-war Europe swiftly retreated from the prophetic dreams of the peacemaking to a tawdry reality of dictatorship, ethnic division, depression, trade conflicts, fascism and war.

> *The First World War led to the second and inter-war Europe swiftly retreated from the prophetic dreams of the peacemaking to a tawdry reality of dictatorship, ethnic division, depression, trade conflicts, fascism and war*

Adolf Hitler: Wilsonian?

The person who dominates our comprehension of inter-war Europe and thereby misleads us is Adolf Hitler. The Nazi German dictator was, in some measure, a Wilsonian, given that he was pledged to self-determination for the German nation, in his mind the heroic offspring of the Aryan race. His various coups of the 1930s – the reoccupation of the Rhineland (March 1936), the *Anschluss* (March 1938) with rump Austria, the taking of the Sudetenland (September 1938) from Czechoslovakia (and Prague and the rest of the country in March 1939) and the seizure of Memel from Lithuania (annexed in March 1939) and Danzig from Poland (September 1939) – each can be read as bringing Germans home to the nation. Aspects of this policy continued in the pursuit of *Volksdeutsche* further east during the war and in negotiation of population exchange from the South Tyrol with his Italian ally to the south. Hitler stands as the epitome of a politician determined to rule all his nationals and to hell, literally, with those who did not belong to Germany, whether they lived inside or outside existing national borders. He is the most terrible simplifier of the practice of seeing the world as constituted by us and the non-national 'other'. His Germany went the furthest (so far) in pushing the total national-ization of human empathy.

Ernest Gellner

Perhaps the most influential theorist of the nation in the aftermath of the Nazi defeat was Ernest Gellner, a sociologist and social anthropologist rather than a historian. A long list of books and articles sketched his views, with his *Thought and Change: The Nature of Human Society* (1964, London: Weidenfeld and Nicolson) and *Nations and Nationalism* (1983, Ithaca, NY: Cornell University Press) being the most significant.

Born in Paris in 1925, Gellner, in what is a familiar tale among students of nations and nationalism, grew up in a secularized Jewish family in the Prague of the 1930s, in 1939 escaping the Holocaust and in 1944–45 enrolling in the Czech army and seeing military service in France. After the defeat of Nazi fascism, he made a brilliant career in the UK, notably at the London School of Economics and Cambridge. Eventually, after the fall of communism in 1993, two years before his death, he returned to Prague, where he ran the Centre for the Study of Nationalism at the Central European University, funded by George Soros.

Gellner ranged widely and he was not one to be cabined, cribbed or confined by the borders of academic disciplines, all the more because he was aware of living among many nationalisms but always at their edge rather than with full 'belonging'. Building on the work of many of his academic predecessors, Gellner sought to separate one version of nationalism from another in a more complex and nuanced manner than Hans Kohn had done, with his simple division into a 'good' western European political nationalism and a 'bad' eastern European one, dabbling too fervently in race and other overheated ideas. In his final and posthumously published work, *Nationalism* (1997, New York: New York University Press), Gellner, with a sociologist's fondness for categories, identified four different zones of national development and five transitional phases in the process of change. Like Kohn, he found agrarian societies to be perpetually pre-national and, like Hobsbawm, but lacking the Marxist's animus, he believed that the forgers of political and cultural ideas, those who filled the bureaucracies that flourished mightily in all the modern states, played a leading part in sketching the different nationalities into existence. Nationalism, Gellner concluded, did not reflect 'the awakening of nations to self-consciousness'; instead, it invented nations where they did not exist. Gellner thus remained highly unconvinced by the views, most amply expressed by his sometime student Anthony D. Smith, that the ethnic sense was genuinely possessed of ancient origins. For Gellner, rather, modernization created nations and nationalism, even while nations and nationalism were the political hallmarks of modernity. Nationalism, he argued, was thus always at root a 'sentiment', an idea. The step from Gellner to Anderson's imagined community is not a large one.

> Always a critic of socialism, especially the 'really existing' Soviet kind in eastern Europe, Gellner, ostentatiously 'apolitical' in his stance on much contemporary debate, had none of Hobsbawm's fondness for socialist internationalism. At the same time, he was rather perplexed by the Zionist project and less convinced than were a number of his elders that Israel stood for civilization in the Middle East and the Arabs for barbarism.

Self-determination and its discontents

But for all his 'madness' (itself an unhelpful term since it implies that Hitler cannot be understood and is 'othered' from us), the Nazi Führer was scarcely alone as the heir of Versailles. A telling map is easily drawn in this regard. By the end of 1938, not one European state outside the western fringe of Norway, Sweden, Denmark, Britain and Eire, France and the Low Countries survived as both liberal and national. Rather, from Finland to Greece and across to Portugal, everywhere freedom was circumscribed in the alleged interest of the nation. In this swathe of countries, dictatorships, whether overt or covert, ousted parliament, channelled capitalism, destroyed trade unions and infringed the rule of law. Minority groups were persecuted. Anti-Semitism gained purchase, as did anti-communism, whether the result of a virtuous rejection of Stalinism or through a war-mongering horror at dreams of internationalism and equality. A fascist understanding of the world took root and blossomed among elites, intellectuals and

Dictatorships, whether overt or covert, ousted parliament, channelled capitalism, destroyed trade unions and infringed the rule of law

quite a few of the masses. And behind the political events lay the structure of ethnic difference. Censuses reported that in Poland (1931) 69 per cent of the population used Polish as their first or 'native' tongue; in Czechoslovakia (merging Czechs and Slovaks) (1930) 67 per cent spoke 'Czechoslovak'; in Yugoslavia (1931) 77 per cent spoke 'Serbocroat' (but the conflict between Serbs and Croats remained fundamental); in Romania (1930) 72 per cent spoke Romanian;[12] each of these tallies was likely to exaggerate the claims of the ruling group.

Self-determination and its discontents: (i) Romania

Of the societies unable to manage the marriage of liberalism and nationalism, Romania was the epitome. This poor peasant country – in 1930, almost 80 per cent of the population drew their income from the land, even though Romania boasted rich (but foreign-owned) oil and other mineral resources[13] – was, through meagre military virtue of its own, a victor of the Great War. In the peacemaking it annexed Bessarabia on its borders with Russia and absorbed Transylvania, a territory with many Magyar-speaking inhabitants and quite a few 'Saxon' Germans to its west. Anxieties about identity were enhanced by what nationalists concocted as the usable past, portraying the country as a 'bulwark of Latinity', buffeted by a sea of Slavs.[14] Anti-Semitism was deeply engrained before 1914, with urban dwellers, for example, believing they could ceremoniously throw Jews into the local river if they happened to pass in freezing January.[15] As a patriotic poet saluted the hatred, xenophobia and paranoia that were basic components of Romanian nationalism:

He who takes strangers to heart,
May the dogs eat his part,
May the waste eat his home,
May ill-fame eat his name![16]

Given this background, it was no wonder that inter-war Romanian politics were violent and authoritarian. An ostentatiously religious fascist movement, the Legion of the Archangel Michael, flourished – one of its mystical aphorisms was 'the first aspect of Legionary life is death'. New members of the Death Commandos swore their readiness to shed their own blood over bags of 'native' soil. The Legion's popular appeal was, however, thwarted first by the outrageously corrupt King Carol and then, during the Second World War, by the Officer Corps and their chief, Marshal Ion Antonescu. This last was backed by Hitler who, impatient of Balkan peccadilloes and aghast at the 'medieval' and unscientific cruelty of their applied anti-Semitism (Legionaries murdered Jews in the Bucharest abattoir using methods of preparing kosher meat), telegraphed, in reaction to the news of the Legion rising, that it should be suppressed at once: 'I don't need fanatics. I need a healthy Rumanian army.'[17]

Self-determination and its discontents: (ii) the Spains

It would be a mistake to leave the impression that eastern Europeans were alone in preferring to identify in an 'integral' fashion with the nation. In western Europe, the 'old nation' of Spain collapsed into bloody civil war in 1936. The battle was a complex contest, with universal Catholicism arrayed on one side and universal Marxism, in various versions, on the other. It was this universalism that encouraged international volunteers from left and right, as well as the intervention of fascist Italy and Nazi Germany in favour of the insurgents and the Stalinist USSR for the republicans. Nonetheless, the battle was fought above all for national identity, with the army (ironically with much of its own nationalism forged in Spain's brutal colonial wars in Morocco) and some fascists groups on the victorious right demanding a Spain that was one and indivisible. The left lacked such unity, with the patriotism of many partially contradicted by anarchist localism or by the proto-nationalism of the Basques and Catalans, people who wanted autonomy for themselves. Pablo Picasso's great painting *Guernica*, destined to become the cherished image of the democratic comprehension of war, recorded the Nazi German fire-bombing of the small town that symbolized Basque aspirations to be free. It therefore combined the universalist ideology of anti-fascism with a commentary on the tyranny of exclusionist, integral nationalism.

Self-determination and its discontents: (iii) the United Kingdom

'Great Britain' (its name expressing some of the ambiguity about the role of nationalism in its islands and empire) had been a society where, for the most part, evocations of nationalism were more muted than they were elsewhere. Even in the debates before 1914 about 'degeneration', the authors of *Scouting for Boys*, worrying that the 'downfall of [classical] Rome' was about to be repeated on British shores, placed the blame on 'the decline of good citizenship and the want of energetic patriotism',[18] not on active nationalism. So, too, in the inter-war period, Oswald Mosley, despite his considerable talents and ruthlessness, did not manage to slot the British Union of Fascists into the political mainstream (even though there were plenty of 'fellow-travellers of the Right' scattered across British society). As rulers of a world-ranging empire and themselves uncertain whether the nationalism to be pursued at home should be British or English (Scots, Welsh and Irish), the British leadership mostly opted for a cosily self-important and arrogant separation of the nation from what Tory prime minister Stanley Baldwin contentedly labelled the 'raving world' outside.[19] This spirit made appeasement, in A.J.P. Taylor's wonderfully arch phrase, a 'triumph of all that was best and most enlightened in British life'[20] and ensured, in September 1938, that Czechoslovakia, the one state in Central Europe then with surviving claims to being a liberal democracy, would be abandoned to Nazi attack.

The British leadership mostly opted for a cosily self-important and arrogant separation of the nation from the 'raving world' outside

One explanation for the relatively benign functioning of nationalism in inter-war Britain and of that country's relative immunity to the appeal of fascism is that those social groups who staffed fascist movements in Italy and Germany were employed in

New perils lurked, however, as the increasing difficulties London faced in managing India, once local nationalists had emerged and begun to organize, were demonstrating

running the British Empire. They were not available forcibly to nationalize socialists at home because they were controlling the lives of millions of subject peoples abroad. Even on the world-circling main, new perils lurked, however, as the increasing difficulties London faced in managing India, once local nationalists had emerged and begun to organize, were demonstrating.

Self-determination and its discontents: (iv) Japan

But the country that had adopted with greatest fervour a non-European version of the nation and its purpose was Japan – imperial Japan, as it was called. Even in recent times and after the Japanese acceptance of liberal democracy (with coaching from its American occupiers) after 1945, quite a few firms begin their workers' days with ceremonies saluting 'the unique features of Japanese society', while a still guilelessly racist researcher in 1978 maintained that he had been able to record his fellow citizens' 'unique' brain structure.[21] Japanese nationalism has not been fully cured of the practice of dividing the world into the foreign them and the national us.

With the Meiji Restoration in 1868, Japan had initiated its course towards modernity at much the same time as Italy and Germany. The rulers of the country quickly committed themselves to catching up with the 'west' and, especially, the USA, at first with some innocence. In the 1870s, one reformer urged: 'Our meagre tongue, which can never be of any use outside of our islands, is doomed to yield to the domination of the English tongue, especially when the power of steam and electricity shall have pervaded the land.'[22]

But such modesty was soon replaced by a desire to win 'the foremost position in the entire world'[23] and by imperial expansion. In 1910 Japan annexed Korea, with a leading and relatively liberal Tokyo paper declaring: 'The world can enjoy peace only when all countries reach the same level of civilization. It cannot permit such a thing as low civilization countries.'[24] Over the following decades, hundreds of thousands of Korean workers were forcibly moved to Japan (in 1945 resident Koreans tallied an estimated two million), where they joined the caste minority of the *Burakumin* (they numbered about a million in 1920) and the native *Ainu* as inferiors excluded from most of the benefits of national economic growth.[25]

During the decade that led up to the Second World War, with Japan's occupation of Manchuria from 1931 and its full-scale attack on China in 1937, the country grew steadily more authoritarian. The imperial regime's 'thought control' was effected through an expression of the nation in the so-called *kokutai*. This credo, affirming the uniqueness, superiority and timelessness of all aspects of Japanese life, practical and spiritual, had been formulated in an imperial rescript on education (1890) and was mystically embodied in succeeding emperors. As a manual of patriotic education put it in 1937: 'the unbroken line of Emperors, receiving the Oracle of the Founder of the Nation, reign eternally over the Japanese Empire. There is one immutable and

> *In Japan, nationalism, racism and imperialism fused and could be deployed rhetorically, despite massive economic and social change, to claim that political interests and systems were permanent and continuity real*

eternal *kokutai*.'[26] In Japan, nationalism, racism and imperialism fused and could be deployed rhetorically, despite massive economic and social change, to claim that political interests and systems were permanent and continuity real. The mixture also drove the country into aggressive war against the USA and the western imperial powers and against Japan's Asian neighbours.

The Second World War

It is true that Europe was at its darkest as a continent in the 1930s and that the rest of the world was scarcely filled with light. While the nations chafed each other and while politicians plotted war and destruction, much progress was nonetheless made and, for many citizens of their various states, the gain could be ascribed to the nation. The worldwide depression spread from the collapse of Wall Street in October 1929 and often prompted a withdrawal from free-trade arrangements in favour of some type of 'autarky' or economic nationalism. Yet, by the end of the 1930s, economies were advancing again, with F.D. Roosevelt providing a model of enlightened government intervention that was destined to expand with the 'welfare nation states' that would be secured after 1945 as a reward to the masses for waging 'people's wars'. Science continued to find solutions to ancient problems; the population of the world grew exponentially; in most places, life expectancy increased. The opportunity for leisure and holidays opened to new social groups, and sport became an activity where national passion could be channelled into the absorbing but apparently harmless arena of athletic competition between the nations. The

Wilsonian recipe may have been failing in Europe and struggling in the rest of the world but optimists could still find value in it, if it was managed peacefully, fairly and without jingoist fanfare.

Here was some hope for the future but, in September 1939, there was at first a rather phoney (except for the viciously attacked Poles) war and, over the next two years leading to the Japanese assault on Pearl Harbor, the conflict expanded to be the Second World War, the appalling conflict summed up in the dire words 'Auschwitz' and 'Hiroshima'. The Second World War led to the death of between 50 and 100 million people (the tally is highly imprecise in the USSR, Asia and the developing world, where national tallying was per force weak). At least half of those slaughtered were civilians, with the Nazis pursuing to the bitter end their bogus racial science in seeking to eliminate certainly European and perhaps global Jewry. Up to six million Jews died in German-occupied Europe, while, in the USSR, perhaps 19 million civilians (and 10 million soldiers) perished, the majority at the hands of the invading Nazis after June 1941, but millions also the victims of that country's own brutal regime.

In these holocausts lies the most familiar image of the war today. Yet the overall Second World War also needs analysis as a series of little, often local, conflicts, where racial or politico-economic ideology was less evident than was more straightforwardly national conflict. Yugoslavia, the most ethnically divided product of the Wilsonian peacemaking, became the nub of multiple civil wars where the field was commanded from one day to the next by Nazis, Italian fascists, Croat *Ustasha* (perhaps the most murderous 'little fascism'), Slovene, Serb and Bosnian Muslim collaborators with the Nazi-fascist new order, royalist

Serb cetniks and communist partisans. Yugoslavia may have stood at the epicentre of death but hellish little wars raged through every nation state or ex-state.

Ethnic cleansings and national holocausts for all

The battles did not reliably end when Hitler and Mussolini were killed in April 1945 and when Nazi-fascism was defeated. Rather, the peace that was achieved only gradually in Europe was accompanied, as in 1919, by vast territorial change, with the vengeful USSR advancing its borders west and driving Poland to annex German lands in compensation. Border changes inevitably demanded the recasting of some national identities and a new wrenching of history to reforge the nation's pretensions to be eternal. Much more than in 1919, the war also resulted in massive ethnic cleansing. More than 10 million Germans were driven out of their centuries old residence in eastern European back to a truncated Germany, itself soon split for two generations into a capitalist, liberal democrat, western version and a communist and 'totalitarian' East Germany. The Germans were not alone. Rather, even as it was denounced as the result of wicked racism, the war ironically hastened the nationalization of the masses in many places where the process was still incomplete in 1939. For all the lip service they gave to internationalism as they fell under Soviet hegemony during the Cold War, each state in eastern Europe was now determined not to countenance large ethnic minorities. In the aftermath of the war, Poland expelled almost half a million 'Ruthenians' or Ukrainians to the USSR. Greece, as it engaged in its own brutal Civil War (1944–45; 1947–49), shunted 15 000 'Chams' (Albanian-speaking Muslims) into Albania and pitilessly purged its Macedonian Slav population. With such persecutions repeated in many other places, it is reckoned that some 46 million east and central Europeans had some refugee experience between 1939 and 1948,[27] and the still Eurocentric international bodies did not begin to count the homeless of Asia and Africa until the 1960s.

George Mosse

George Mosse (1918–99) was one of the great liberal historians of the modern nation. His book *The Nationalization of the Masses: Political Symbolism and Mass Movements from the Napoleonic Wars through the Third Reich* (1975, New York: H. Fertig) was like Benedict Anderson's in providing a catchphrase for much later commentary.

Mosse came from a rich, successful and assimilated bourgeois Jewish-German family, where, as he put it, his religion was 'a matter of lifestyle rather than faith'. Such liberal capitalist 'Jews of German culture' were tragically destined to run directly into the horror of Nazism. Mosse himself avoided the worst fate by escaping the Final Solution along a track that carried him first to sanctuary in fascist Italy, then to education in Britain and finally to the USA and an academic career in that country. From a chair at the University of Wisconsin, Mosse pondered the meaning of the nation, while never ceasing to watch anxiously over the perhaps new, perhaps old story of the embattled post-1948 state of Israel. In his old age, when identity politics became the US norm, Mosse came out as a homosexual.

Mosse's main research focused on modern Germany, pondering the question how this nation, a pinnacle of European culture, should 'go to Auschwitz'. How could it, during the Second World War, perpetrate genocide without much sign of objection from its people? His answer to these questions went back to the eighteenth century. Then, the idea of the nation had found its distinct and modern form. The great positive insight of the Enlightenment was that thereafter men and women should not have to be in thrall to an imponderable god. Rather, by harnessing science they could perfect themselves. The pre-modern world was irrational; the modern one must become ever more rational and scientific. 'Progress' sprang from that equation.

So much may have been the expectation of the *philosophes* at their most optimistic but, commented Mosse with a pessimism that owed something to his life experience, the irrational is always with us. During the eighteenth century, one god may have been ceremoniously buried, but another crept in the window of the soul. While human beings agreed that they should no longer bow to monarchs, acting as the vice-regents of the old god on earth and magically bearing his blessings, they began to harbour instead the god of the nation. The accoutrements of pre-modern religion – relics, saints, hymns, church sacraments and services – were replaced by flags, heroes, anthems and the ceremonies of the nation. Modern men and women were schooled from infancy by the myths of national 'history'. National display, growing ever more complex in the nineteenth century and reinforced by the First World War and its subsequent urgent need to give meaning to death and 'sacrifice' by 'ordinary soldiers', was taking on a life of its own. The nation's seductive promise of secure and eternal identity swept through the nineteenth- and twentieth-century world and plumbed its fearful abyss in the swastika flag, the marching cohorts of the SA and SS, the Nazi chants, the guttering torches of a Nuremberg party meeting, the gas of Treblinka and the merciless pit-killings of the Eastern Front. Avoiding much commentary on 'good' nationalism, which he may have assumed existed in the Anglo-Saxon world and in Israel, Mosse pointed sadly to the ways in which myths move mountains. The idea and practice of the nation, he maintained, fomented war and unleashed destruction as readily in modern times as once had the irrationalities and fanaticisms of pre-industrial societies.

In his movingly sensitive study of the fate of German and Jewish children during the war, Nick Stargardt has exposed how the horror of war on land and from the skies further narrowed empathy among the Germans, a cruel concentration encouraged by Nazi propaganda enhancing the earlier processes of national-ization where people came to believe that only their national fellows mattered. Eventually, German civilians confined them-selves to despairing nightly prayers that the bombs fall on some-one, anyone, else. Ironically, therefore, 'they were hollowing out that feeling of national community which [Nazi] propaganda about vengeance and retaliation struggled to revive during the daytime'.[28] In the abyss of 1945, the family could no longer auto-matically merge into the nation.

Although the topic has not been researched thoroughly, this potential partial disillusion with the nation, given the direct suf-fering from the war, the conflict's presence on the skin of almost every continental European at some time between 1939 and 1945, may help to explain the growth of the European Union in the post-war period and the ability of this supranational organ-ization to win public sympathy, despite its evident failings. It may also be the cause, ever since the defeat of Nazism, of the lack of enthusiasm in most of Europe towards new wars. Japan has fol-lowed what may be a similar line. By contrast, those combatant nations that did not directly experience occupation and the passage of battle fronts, places therefore less attuned to the problematic of the nation – the USA, Australia, the UK – have remained readier to launch themselves into battle.

Another result of the war, although it took a few extra years to achieve, deserves notice. In 1948, the Jews, the prime victims of the Nazis along with the Soviets but themselves guiltless of

Israel arose in the Middle East, in territory that had once been weakly governed by the Ottoman Empire, in what nineteenth-century Zionists had begun to think of as the land of Zion

'Stalinism', won a nation state of their own. Rather than being in Europe, where the other subject peoples of the pre-modern empires had erected their states, Israel arose in the Middle East, in territory that had once been weakly governed by the Ottoman Empire, in what nineteenth-century Zionists had begun to think of as the land of Zion. The British had possessed a mandate over the place since the First World War. They called it Palestine and, through the inter-war period, had failed to craft a clear method of coping with the violent differences that surfaced between the surviving Arab or Palestinian inhabitants, those Jews determined or lucky enough to be granted the right to settle there, and, for that matter, the European Christian churches that still sought recognition for themselves in what they deemed the 'Holy Places'.

Israel and its nationalisms will be dealt with more fully later when we consider the framing of nations in immigrant societies. But, for the moment, one matter should be underlined since, from 1945, it has become a dominant and inevitable theme in every nationalist discourse. The Nazis had sought to extirpate Jewry, and those who did not agree with their ideology had proved slow and inadequate in frustrating and defeating their appalling purpose. As a result, if the Jews did indeed compose a nation, then it was highly logical that they should possess a national homeland and a nation state. If any nation has an historical right to exist, Israel does.

The idea, as still enunciated from time to time by such fanatical anti-Semites as, in 2006, the president of Iran, Mahmoud Ahmadinejad, that the Israeli Jews should pack up and go home to Europe is intolerable. Yet the very success of Israel did carry a dam-

> *If the Jews did indeed compose a nation, then it was highly logical that they should possess a national homeland and a nation state. If any nation has an historical right to exist, Israel does*

aging message to the world, endlessly and mindlessly repeated in today's media. As Peter Novick has put it in his account of the historicizing of the 'Holocaust' (as by the 1960s it was coming to be known), after 'Auschwitz', 'Jews defined themselves by their history of victimization'. They had won the 'gold medal' in victimhood. By demanding an absolute acceptance of the idea that their suffering was unique, they drove any discussion about Israeli politics into silence or the absolute. Criticism and nuance became impossible: 'First stop, an anti-Semitic joke, last stop, Treblinka.'[29]

Meanwhile, in unspoken imitation of this process, a slew of other nations sought to gain the silver or bronze medal in the increasingly energetic contest to be victims. As the Serb treatment of Kosovo proves, great 'national' defeats, safely located in the past, have long been grist to the nationalist mill. But the way that the Holocaust took over all the Second World Wars and ensured that the terrible time between 1939 and 1945 must own to a single historical meaning made its message universal in a highly distorted and ironically nationalized manner. Now all ethnic groups envied and emulated Jewish victimhood with the present message that any rejection of their ideas or the blocking of their purpose were wickedly and intolerably repeating past sin and murder. Now it became ever more necessary that each nation was utterly united and singular, and so more integral, since every member bore the memory of a time of persecution and carried the determination to prevent it happening again. Now more than ever nations honoured their dead but did not mourn those they had killed. By this rhetorical means, and occurring structurally rather than through individual act, the Second World War of deathly combat between races and national groups but also between ideologies, classes (and even genders) was redefined in a fashion that paved the way for new, and again potentially absolute, national and racial rivalries.

Notes

1   R.S. Wortman, '"Invisible threads": the historical imagery of the Romanov tercentenary', *Russian History*, 1989, 16, pp. 390, 392–3, 400–403.

2   H.F. Jahn, *Patriotic Culture in Russia during World War I* (1995, Ithaca, NY: Cornell University Press), p. 173.

3   J.A. Sandborn, 'Unsettling the empire: violent migrations and social disaster in Russia during the First World War', *Journal of Modern History*, 2005, 77, p. 292.

4   See R.J.B. Bosworth, *Mussolini's Italy: Life under the Dictatorship 1915–1945* (2005, London: Allen Lane), pp. 37–92.

5   A. Ventrone, *La seduzione totalitaria: Guerra, modernità, violenza politica (1914–1918)* (2003, Rome: Donzelli), p. 26.

6   *Ibid.* pp. 38, 110–11, 125.

7   See, for example, W. Wilson, *A History of the American People* (1902, New York: Harper).

8   C. Seymour, *The Intimate Papers of Colonel House*, vol. IV (1926, New York: Houghton Mifflin), p. 294.

9   A. Heckscher, *The Politics of Woodrow Wilson* (1956, New York: Harper), p. 352.

10 J.M. Keynes, *The Economic Consequences of the Peace* (1920, London: Macmillan), p. 38.

11 See especially A.J. Mayer, *Wilson versus Lenin: Political Origins of the New Diplomacy 1917–1918* (1959, New Haven, CT: Yale University Press); *Politics and Diplomacy of Peacemaking: Containment and Counter-Revolution at Versailles, 1918–1919* (1968, London: Weidenfeld and Nicolson).

12 Figures adapted from J. Rothschild, *East Central Europe between the Wars* (1974, Seattle, WA: University of Washington Press), pp. 36, 89, 203, 284.

13 N.M. Nagy-Talavera, *The Green Shirts and Others: A History of Fascism in Hungary and Rumania* (1970, Stanford, CA: Stanford University Press), pp. 17, 30.

14 For evocation, see T. Tittoni, *Questioni del giorno* (1928, Milan: Treves), p. 56.

15 M. Parkinson, *Twenty Years in Romania* (1921, London: George Allen and Unwin), pp. 112–13.

16 E. Weber, citing Mihail Eminescu, 'Romania', in H. Rogger and E. Weber (eds), *The European Right: A Historical Profile* (1965, London: Weidenfeld and Nicolson), p. 507. Eminescu apparently hated Greeks even more than he did Jews.

17 Nagy-Talavera, *The Green Shirts and Others*, pp. 290, 326.

18 Quoted by P. Wilkinson, 'English youth movements, 1908–1930', *Journal of Contemporary History*, 1969, 4, p. 10.

19 S. Baldwin, *Service of our Lives* (1937, London: Hodder and Stoughton), p. 24.

20 A.J.P. Taylor, *The Origins of the Second World War* (1964, Harmondsworth: Penguin), pp. 7–8, 235.

21 R. Mouer and Y. Sugimoto, *Images of Japanese Society: A Study in the Structure of Social Reality* (1986, London: KPI), pp. 51, 170.

22 I.P. Hall, *Mori Arinori* (1973, Cambridge, MA: Harvard University Press), p. 189.

23 *Ibid.* p. 399.

24 M. Weiner, *The Origins of the Korean Community in Japan 1910–1923* (1989, Manchester: Manchester University Press), p. 21.

25 K.W. Tong, 'Korea's forgotten atomic bomb victims', *Bulletin of Concerned Asian Scholars*, 1991, 23, pp. 31–2.

26 C. Gluck, *Japan's Modern Myths: Ideology in the Late Meiji Period* (1985, Princeton, NJ: Princeton University Press), p. 283.

27 M. Mazower, *Dark Continent: Europe's Twentieth Century* (1998, Harmondsworth: Penguin), pp. 217, 239.

28 N. Stargardt, *Witnesses of War: Children's Lives under the Nazis* (2005, London: Jonathan Cape), p. 252.

29 P. Novick, *The Holocaust in American Life* (1999, Boston, MA: Houghton Mifflin), pp. 8–9, 171, 178.

CHAPTER 5

International Marxism and the nation

IN HIS ACCOUNT OF THE 1905 revolution in the Russian Empire, the then still independent Marxist revolutionary Leon Trotsky reserved some of his choicest epithets for the Union of Russian People. These new patriots and nationalists were, he maintained, composed of the 'savage scum of the taverns and the convict labour gangs'. They were the hirelings of Tsar Nicholas II, a bunch of 'pogromists and thieves', worthy agents of a ruler who was himself 'dull-witted and scared, an all-powerful nonentity, the prey of prejudices worthy of an Eskimo, the royal blood in his veins poisoned by all the vices of many generations'.[1] Trotsky, a self-consciously brilliant young Jewish intellectual, was

Trotsky was marshalling his understandings and prejudices with care. Nationalists, and the monarch who in an emergency saw fit to fund them, were brutal, uprooted, corrupt and stupid, no better than savages

marshalling his understandings and prejudices with care. Nationalists, and the monarch who in an emergency saw fit to fund them, were brutal, uprooted, corrupt and stupid, no better than savages. Their ideas, their morality and their future were laughably inferior to that of any decent Marxist and worker. They needed to be opposed and destroyed as the world moved inexorably towards its happier and international future. When Marxism won its predestined global victory, the nations would wither away; the era of their significance would prove fleeting. How did Marxists entertain such hopes and why did they prove so delusive?

The International and the nations

Among more decorous socialists than Trotsky, the official line before 1914 similarly clung to the view that socialism crossed borders with facility and as readily subjugated nationalist passions. In France, the Parti Ouvrier, hard-nosed in its determination to bring the benefits of 'gas and water' socialism to those municipalities that it was beginning to govern, often expressed its allegiance to 'the common interests of the entire proletariat, independently of all nationality'. Despite their local roots, the Guesdists, as they were familiarly known, were well to the fore in the meetings of the 'Second International', the body that brought together socialists of all countries, promising, in the event of capitalist war, to proclaim a general strike that would stop warmongers in their tracks in every combatant nation. Then would be made plain the superiority of class over nationhood.

Yet, for all their Marxist knowledge and commitment, the Guesdists were time and again forced to acknowledge that national identity was becoming an ever more powerful factor in ample sectors of life. Despite their socialism, they and very many of their fraternal comrades in other European countries half admitted that they belonged to their nation. Even when meetings of the International were at their least formal, national differences kept surfacing. As a Russian delegate remembered the August 1910 congress at Copenhagen when, one evening, a boat trip and dinner were arranged:

The buffet was an enormous success; corks popped, there was an incessant clatter of plates and the staff scuttled about. The Germans raised great tankards of dark beer and shouted 'Prosit!' The French and Italians clinked glasses of burgundy and chianti. The English slowly drank their ale and whisky-and-soda. There was even vodka for the Russian comrades. It was all noisy, crowded and somewhat stuffy. Next came singing and dancing. Each delegation gave of its best. There was a competition between the nations. We Russians were far from coming in last. A.A. Kollontay was a tremendous success.[2]

International revolution in Russia

The outbreak only four years later of the First World War and the failure at that moment of the International, with the best organized and most conceptually sophisticated of its members, the German Social Democrat party, agreeing to vote credits for its imperial government, laid starkly bare the fissure separating socialism's theoretical internationalism from the reality of national loyalty. The general strike indeed proved a general non-sense as its critics had always prophesied. Nor with the course of the war was the socialist dilemma of how to relate to the nation resolved. In October 1917, the Bolsheviks of Russia, purists who had opposed the Romanov Empire's war from its inception, overthrew the provisional government, seizing power in the name of the global proletariat. Yet even in this act, contradiction lurked. In occupying the Winter Palace in Petrograd, Lenin and his friends were trying to speed the course of history towards world revolution faster than orthodox Marxism had wanted. Deciding that 'backward' Russia constituted the 'weak link' in the chain of capitalist power, the revolutionary government pushed Russia, or, to be more accurate, the Russias, into a prominence that German or French socialists had not foreseen. In the birth throes of the Soviets, the prospect of 'socialism in one country' and of an adaptation of Marxism to a national setting can be read between the lines of the pronouncements about a global new beginning.

Lenin and his friends were trying to speed the course of history towards world revolution faster than orthodox Marxism had wanted

In noting this situation it is not necessary to follow anticommunist zealots into the crude thesis that Bolshevism was always a variant of 'national socialism'. Rather, throughout the history of the USSR as it came to be known, Soviet Marxist ideas were destined to twist and turn in their comprehension of nationality and in their planning for it. Nowadays the dismal economic, social and cultural failures of the Soviet state and its whimpering away at the end of the 1980s, when it lost on every front of the second Cold War, make it easy to deride or ignore Soviet history. Yet, for many decades after 1917, the USSR did offer, at least in theory, alternative ways to approach national identity from those adopted in the capitalist world. Furthermore, the eventual failure of the various Soviet lines about the nation is a major explanation why the USSR proved such a pushover during its last days. Of similar significance is the fact that Yugoslavia, the most multinational society in that eastern Europe dominated for two

The dismal economic, social and cultural failures of the Soviet state and its whimpering away at the end of the 1980s, when it lost on every front of the second Cold War, make it easy to deride or ignore Soviet history

generations by the Soviets after 1945, also proved unable to escape its national contests. In the 1990s, Yugoslavia collapsed into vicious and multiple national civil wars, signalling to all but Fukuyama that the end of the Soviet experiment was not entailing the end of history. As they converted their control of the Winter Palace into rule over most of the ex-Romanov empire, the Soviets may have thought their past, present and future were defined by class. But, in much practice of 'really existing socialism' before and after 1945, the key element was to be the nation.

Stalin and the nation

When the Bolsheviks formed their first government, the post of commissar of nationalities went to the figure among the generally cosmopolitan, intellectual and, to quite a degree, Jewish party leadership who was the least cosmopolitan and intellectual and who was not Jewish. His name was Joseph Stalin and he came from the restless southern border territories of the collapsing empire. His emerging rival and eventual victim Trotsky did not disdain ethnic stereotyping when he depicted Stalin as an 'Asiatic' who blended 'grit, shrewdness, craftiness and cruelty' and completed the damning portrait for his European readers with the comment that Georgia was 'the Spain of the Caucasus', a place with a brutal and brutalised history.[3] A more recent scholar has similarly argued that Stalin was a 'man of the borderlands', always a peasant bandit at heart.[4]

Yet, in his blossoming career among the Bolsheviks, Stalin was also an insider and a populist, evidently a 'man of the people' in a way that Trotsky, Zinoviev, Bukharin and Lenin, 'the Great Headmaster',[5] were not. Back in 1912 Stalin had muttered mutinously, and with a whiff of injured nationalism, that the organization of his comrades in exile was 'not everything and not even the main thing. The main thing is to organize activities in Russia.'[6] Many years later when writing off Bukharin as a nonperson, Stalin lambasted him and his ilk as 'Communist *literati* . . . [who] sat for years in [European] cafes, drank beer, and were nonetheless unable to learn Europe or to understand it'.[7] Compared with such poseurs, Stalin liked it to be known that he was an ordinary Russian Joe. Far and away the most credible and, contrary to the professional anti-communists' pieties, the bleakest account of the rise of 'Stalinism' to Soviet rule sets Stalin's personality into the structures of the 'backwardness', ignorance and cruelty of life and attitudes in all the Russias. In this view, by the 1930s the intellectually sophisticated and

> *Stalin was also an insider and a populist, evidently a 'man of the people' in a way that Trotsky, Zinoviev, Bukharin and Lenin were not*

cosmopolitan Old Bolsheviks, half aware of their own perversion in fighting a permanent hot and cold civil war, had guiltily opted for policies to accelerate the arrival of the 'genuine masses' in authority. Such favouring of workers and peasants allowed a hundred thousand little Stalins to bloom and, in their eager advance towards power, to blast with their popular culture every utopian and intellectual hope held by the revolutionaries before 1917.

What, then, during this process was happening to Marxist internationalism in the USSR? As commissar of nationalities, Stalin had begun with an act of studious propriety. On 14 November 1917, he crossed the narrow sea and addressed at Helsinki a meeting of comrades in the Finnish Social Democratic Party.[8] The new commissar announced that Romanov rule, imposed on the territory in 1809 and, by the late nineteenth century, opposed by such nationalist intellectuals as the composer Jean Sibelius (he composed a 'Karelia suite' with irredentist message), was at an end. Revolution in Petrograd ensured self-determination for all and so guaranteed a lasting national independence in Helsinki. As Stalin explained: 'A nation can organize its life as it sees fit. It has the right to organize its life on the basis of autonomy. It has the right to enter into federal relations with other nations. It has the right to complete secession. Nations are sovereign and all nations are equal.'[9]

During the months that followed, the outbreak of vicious civil war throughout the Russias soon prompted revision of this generous line. Already in January 1918, the commissar of nationalities, confronted by Ukrainian secession, qualified his enthusiasm for ethnic liberation. The principle of self-determination, Stalin now pronounced, 'ought to be understood as the right of self-determination not of the bourgeoisie but of the toiling masses of a given nation. The principle of self-determination ought to be used as a means in the struggle for socialism and it ought to be subordinated to the principles of socialism.'[10] Nations lacking territory were not 'real', the commissar said.[11] Although the Soviets had accepted the independence of Finland, Russian Poland and the Baltic states, and although violent contestation of imperial rule would linger for more than a decade in other parts of the country, the revolution, rather than dissolving the Romanov realm, had restored its lands. Like Nicholas II, Lenin and Stalin were to rule an empire on which the sun was slow to set.

Yet, here, too, the victory in the civil war did not necessarily bring contentment and certainty. Through the 1920s, rival thoughts about the 'nationality problem' continued to exercise the revolutionary leadership. Was revived 'imperial' rule for ever, or just in the short term, until the subject nationalities could ready themselves, or be made ready, for proletarian freedom? How could elites find a way to assist those who were presently 'backward'? Or was the very term 'backwardness' itself patronizing and tyrannous, damnably 'bourgeois', whatever the seeming revolutionary credentials of those in office? Anyway, just what is a nation? In a country with myriad languages and proto-languages, cultures and proto-cultures, how could 'real' nations be given mathematically, geographically and socially 'true' and just borders? How could false nations be discouraged, contained, suppressed or liquidated? The dilemmas set deep into the rule of a Soviet empire that was as troubled by its empire as it was by the task of making socialism and socialists nagged away at policymakers.

The society where the devastating effects of world and civil war, social revolution and famine had scoured deeply (there were an estimated seven million homeless children of uncertain nationality roaming Soviet streets in 1921[12]) and where, as a result, many people were possessed of identities that were potentially dangerous, in need of amendment, lost with the lost records or deliberately obscured was in its deepest sinews nervous and uneasy. Hazy about the seemingly simple issue of whom individuals might be, the citizens of the USSR had their resulting paranoia exacerbated by the fear that the path to socialism could at best be detected through a glass darkly and by the evidence that national division and difference were constantly distorting and undermining any socialist (let alone any internationalist) achievement.

Such matters should not be overstated. Quite a few of the issues raised by imperial governance confronted liberal capitalist empires, too, when in time they grew doubtful about the virtue or reward of ruling subject peoples; such dilemmas continue to worry the contemporary USA. Yet, in no society of the twentieth century was the combination

The issues raised by imperial governance confronted liberal capitalist empires, too, when in time they grew doubtful about the virtue or reward of ruling subject peoples; such dilemmas continue to worry the contemporary USA

of power and passion on the one hand and falsification and manipulation on the other more troubling in its effects than it was in the USSR. The style of government in the USSR arose not because 'the Bolsheviks imposed their blueprint on society'; rather, it sprang from the fact that 'they could not'.[13] With every passing year, the USSR leadership grew more depressed, frustrated and angry about this failure to convert utopian dreams into anything that bore connection with reality. And at the epicentre of the USSR's contradictions, the problem of the nation refused to vanish.

The Finnish case

Language policy offers a telling example. If Finland now was 'free' – the country's politics retained an authoritarian cast throughout the inter-war period and, during the 1930s, a slew of Germanophile nationalists flirted with a native fascism – the adjacent lands of what became the Soviet Republic of Karelia were ethnically disputed or disputable. The Finns made their last military incursion into the region as late as 1922.[14] Despite the possibility of irredentism, for two decades after 1917 the official language in the Soviet Republic was nonetheless Finnish; in 1932, 99.6 per cent of local schoolchildren were studying in this tongue and the region's 'finlandization' seemed all but complete. Anthropologists and linguists, each working in disciplines for the moment favoured by the Soviet state, had, however, reckoned that the inhabitants of the territory spreading north to the White and Barents seas actually spoke not Finnish but Vote, Izhor (sometimes called Ingrian or Ingermanland Finnish), Veps and Karelian, each of which could be called a language.

The Great Purge of 1937 shook this kaleidoscope and, for a time, a new pattern emerged. Edward Gylling (1881–1938), the previous boss of the Republic, fell along with many other Old Bolsheviks and was killed. His demise signalled an abrupt turn in language policy; now, the use of Finnish was deemed an error, un-socialist. From 1 January 1938, children were to be schooled in some more acceptable national tongue, while the speaking in the playground of Finnish, condemned as a 'fascist language,' was banned. The Finnish translations of Marx, Engels and Lenin were assembled and publicly burned. Under the impulse of the linguist D.V. Bubrikh, for the moment a 'Stalinist' but in 1932 the advocate of the creation of a single world socialist tongue, Karelian, written in Cyrillic, was 'modernized', with its cases cut from 13 (in 1932), to 12 (in 1937) and then to nine. While this pedantic effort to engineer human speech patterns proceded, Karelians, as an academic analyst has wryly noted, 'themselves could not understand their new official language'.[15]

The twists did not cease. In April 1940, after the hard-fought Soviet victory in the Winter War against Finland, Karelian was replaced by Finnish again and the 'little nationality' of the locals was soon being discouraged by the Russian nationalism that became a marked feature of the USSR's Great Patriotic War against Nazism after June 1941. Already, in 1938, schoolchildren were obliged to learn Russian, while, that same year, Russian was elevated to be the sole language of command in the Soviet army.[16] With the denunciation of Stalin by Khrushchev in 1956, however, the eddies reached Karelia and Finnish again took a backward step before instruction in Karelian, while the Republic itself was renamed the Karelian Autonomous Republic instead of the Karelo-Finnish SSR. Thereafter, as Soviet rule became more frozen and gerontocratic, a rough compromise settled into place. At the fall of the USSR, 41 per cent of locals declared that they were Finnish speakers and 51 per cent Karelian, while, from July 1990, the autonomous Karelian republic within the new Russia recognized Veps as the third of its official languages.[17]

First peoples and the Soviet nation

The battles over Karelian were scarcely unique. Indeed, the USSR's arctic zone further to the east made Karelia look ethnically and linguistically simple. Initially the state's approach to the bewildering cultural diversity in these territories was blunt. Difference should be abolished. In 1930, it was typically declared with a telling choice of Marxist metaphor that 'the advanced peoples are tearing along on the rapid locomotive of history . . . At the same time the backward peoples have to "race like the wind" . . . to catch up.'[18] Those who spoke such languages as Nenets, Evenk, Chukchi, Orok and Udege were labelled 'savages' – longstanding Russian folklore, barbarous in its own peremptory misunderstandings, had been convinced that such peoples were guilty of cannibalism and infanticide (and both together), could live in the sea throughout summer and had mouths on top of their heads.[19] In 1928, a long list of 'crimes that constitute survivals of tribalism' were to be extirpated forthwith. As the historian of the area has explained, in words that similarly echo through capitalist European 'native policy' in this era, 'children [in these places] had to relearn how to eat, sleep, talk, dress and be sick, as well as to assimilate to a totally new view of the world and their place in it.'[20] The Soviets, in other words, were trying to forge their Arctic subjects into being 'Soviet new boys and girls' and, in the process, to wipe out their traditional ethnic or national identity. In this instance the 'Stalin revolution' did not lead to a somersault in policy. Rather, by the late 1930s, victory was proclaimed in the process of assimilation (however much beneath the surface opposition to the Soviet system roiled) and, lest there be too much testing of the matter, ethnography was banned as a 'bourgeois pseudoscience'.[21] Stalinist rule had decided that it did not want to know about lingering ethnic differences in these parts of the USSR.

Stalinist rule had decided that it did not want to know about lingering ethnic differences in these parts of the USSR

The case of the Ukraine

If 'native policy' was a vexing issue for Soviet planners, then the fate of greater nationalities was still harder to frame with Marxist justice, certainty and science. The territory of the Ukraine, for example, had fallen under Romanov rule in the mid seventeenth century and, well before that time, the city of Kiev, first citadel of 'Rus', had provided historical moments that were later depicted as heralding the 'dawn of Russian history'. After the fall of the USSR, the emergence of a Ukrainian nation state would be bolstered in some circles with the sort of outrageous claims that might make any sensible citizen gag. Then it was suggested that the Ukraine was the original homeland of all the Indo-European peoples, Ukrainians were Aryans in 'blood', 'Ukrainian-Sanskrit' was the mother of all Indo-European languages and the Ukrainian tongue was actually 25 000 years old, being therefore 'the language of the world aristocracy'. It was alleged that the ancestors of the Ukrainians, known as 'Trypillians', invented the alphabet and the calendar, gave birth to Buddha and Zarathustra (while Christ was of Galician or western Ukrainian descent), and provided the key craftsmen who erected Stonehenge. An ancient but really existing Ukrainian empire ran from the Atlantic to the Pacific, the Amazons were Ukrainian and so was Troy, while Attila was really not a Hun but a Ukrainian. So, of course, were the 'Et rus cans' (and thus all that mattered in the civilization of Rome).

A historian of these matters has warned 'the Ukrainians are not uniquely guilty of historical embellishment' and, sadly, he is correct in his caution.[22] In passing, readers of this book might, however, note the lying that is involved in the Ukrainian national cause and again remind themselves to be sceptical of all nationalist claims about longevity and significance. Certainly, it was only in the nineteenth century, that seed time of the nations, that any credible Ukrainian identity can be seen as emerging or as being invented. In 1844, the satirical writer Nikolai Gogol (now called Mykola Hohol) mused: 'I do not know whether my soul is Ukrainian or Russian.' Those 'Ruthenians' under Habsburg rule in what is now western Ukraine experienced some nationalization during the ensuing decades following the pattern occurring elsewhere in that empire; by the 1890s, a standardized Ukrainian was being taught in some schools and the University of Lvov established a chair in Ukrainian history.[23] Emigrants to the USA and Canada also began to think of themselves in national terms, in that curious but common process of nationalizing after departure from a homeland. But in the Russian-ruled Ukraine, even if the Russian Academy of Sciences agreed that Ukrainian was a language and not a dialect, any serious acknowledgement of national identity won little support until after the Bolshevik revolution, with the official definition of the Tsar's subjects remaining 'people of the lands of Rus'.[24]

One effect of the terrible dislocation of the revolutionary years was that, in 1928 in Vienna, émigrés who admired Germanic culture established a proto-fascist body called the Organization of Ukrainian Nationalists, adopting the somewhat uneasy slogan 'Ukraine does not yet exist but we can create it in our souls'. In 1941, this body would distinguish itself by declaring its determination 'to "vanquish" the Jew from the Ukraine', although its potential Nazi allies remained suspicious of its purpose and doubtful of its popular base.[25] But it was within the USSR that a paradoxical Ukrainian identity was being assembled, both because state-sponsored industrialization was entailing massive urbanization and so assisting those processes that had prompted the nationalization of ex-peasants in many countries further to the west, and because the Soviet regime wanted the Ukraine to be a 'socialist republic', another allegedly equal member in the Union.

Stalin provided the anxious formula that the party in the Ukraine should prove 'national in form, socialist in content'.[26] The emergence of his personality cult and dictatorship by the end of the 1920s coincided with an official line that distanced itself from Romanov disdain for a separate identity in the region. Language usage was actually complex, given the widespread illiteracy and the fact that a majority of locals were either Russian speakers or preferred *Surzhyk*, a tongue blending Russian and Ukrainian and destined never to lose its inferiority as a 'dialect'.[27] As in so many other places before the simplifications required by modernity, very many people spoke more than one language with the usage depending on time and need. Nonetheless, from 1923, the regime demanded that public officials in the Republic learn Ukrainian and try to spread its use. In 1933, as the Soviets' determination to classify its peoples grew ever more neurotic, 60 per cent of Party members there labelled themselves Ukrainian, although only about half of them spoke the 'national' language.

This linguistic preference soon became an error – for quite a few, a fatal error – as the Party line for the locomotive of history switched. The appalling costs of the collectivization campaign, at their worst in the Ukraine, were explained away as the result of a wicked nationalism. The previous party boss, Mykola Skrypnyk, was now damned as a 'national degenerate', leader of the 'nationalist deviation . . . coming close to the counter-revolutionaries, working for the cause of [foreign] intervention' and driven to suicide in a rhetoric and a practice that would grow more familiar in the coming purges.[28] The policymakers in Moscow sought exculpation by nationalizing the terrible events; in their view, Ukrainian plots had blighted an otherwise ideal scenario. Such an interpretation in turn allowed, and allows, Ukrainian nationalists (and some professional anti-communists) to convert the disasters of collectivization into a Soviet or Russian 'genocide' perpetrated on the Ukrainians; in 1993, 12 September was made a national Ukrainian holiday to commemorate the famine of 1932–33, with a death toll that was inevitably set at 'six million'.[29]

The story, after the reappearance of Russian nationalism among the Stalinist leadership during the 1930s, remained complex. Millions of Ukrainians died fighting against the Nazi invader from 1941, many without nationalist intent. Yet the war was 'totalizing' the ethnic divisions of the USSR and so restoring eternity and uniformity to the national groups. Between 1944 and 1946, the secret police detained 110 785 Ukrainian 'bandits', almost always inscribing nationalism on to them.[30] At the same

> *The war was 'totalizing' the ethnic divisions of the USSR and so restoring eternity and uniformity to the national groups*

time, the monumentalization of the war was pursued with enthusiasm or desperation and it, too, reinforced the ethnic categories that, a generation earlier, Old Bolsheviks had wanted to erase. Complications could ensue from the increasing demand that bystanders in the conflict should be damned as no better or even worse than collaborators, while quite a few who sought office or recognition must have had, or must be able to claim to have had, war service and sacrifice.[31] Yet, if 'great Russia' had led the war, all the smaller Russias potentially had something to explain away; the 'greatest moment of history' might not reliably serve their interests.

Soviet nation or nations

Rather than pursuing the flickering history of the place of Ukrainian identity in the Ukrainian Soviet Socialist Republic until the fall of the Soviet system (and a Ukrainianized war did exist until the end, to be taken over by the Ukrainian nation state after 1990), it should be noted how contradictory the ethnic identity of Soviet men and women remained throughout the empire and how Stalinism reinforced the fears and nourished the hatreds involved, especially for those who got their 'nationality' wrong at any given moment amid the oscillations of the Party line. The Stalinist system was another that, in its deepest ideology and practice, was teaching people to hate, and to do so on ethnic grounds.

In one of those paradoxes in which the ever more authoritarian and culturally narrow USSR specialized, the choice of nation was intricate. When the rulers decreed in the 1920s that each citizen needed to opt for an ethnic identity, 172 of such

Unintentionally the Soviet regime was building national allegiances rather more successfully than it was achieving socialism

categories were officially available; by 1939 the number had been cut to 57 'major' nationalities.[32] Unintentionally, then, the Soviet regime was building national allegiances rather more successfully than it was achieving socialism. As ever, the impact on the peoples of the empire was erratic. The selection of nationality had to be made when a citizen turned 16 years. Teenagers by no means had to be bound by their parents' preferences, which, after all, often had been made from multiple possibilities. It was possible to be unlucky. Almost inevitably in a paranoid society such as the USSR, the issuing of compulsory passports with an obliged national category stamped into them entailed 'bad' as well as 'good' nationalities. Both in that regard and in (alleged) class background, which was also obsessively recorded, the classification meant that a 'hierarchy of privileges' was being sought by fair means or foul in so materially deprived a society. Something of the chaos never far from the surface in the USSR is indicated in the statistic that, by 1939, after seven years of police activity, still only 50 out of 162 million Soviets had been properly registered with passports (*kolkhoz* peasants were ineligible until the 1960s).[33] Just how many in this process had decided to fake their identity remains unknown. Nonetheless, already from 1935, ethnic cleansing campaigns were launched against peoples who, by living too near a frontier or for some other historical reason, could be portrayed as potential enemies, the more dangerous when their hostility was 'latent' (even when that word meant nonexistent). During the Great Purge, Poles, Germans, Estonians,

Latvians, Koreans, Chinese, Kurds and Iranians (plus Finns) were removed from the so-called 'border zones' (they had been gazetted back in 1923). Officially, 'national operations' precipitated 36.3 per cent of the killing in 1937–38; the actual figure was probably higher given that the word '*kulak*' often hid ethnic difference.[34]

The ebb and flow of the front in the Great Patriotic War caused further tension. Real or suspected collaboration with the Germans proved fatal for hundreds of thousands of Chechens and other peoples from the Caucasus (while the Nazis sowed their own dissent by reckoning that Georgians and Estonians were Aryan). The war, with its appalling toll of dead in the USSR, acted as a *The war acted as a 'third social revolution', another moment when identities could be made, altered or lost* 'third social revolution', another moment when identities could be made, altered or lost. In the whirlpool of events, it was really no surprise that Stalin, and probably many others, dreamed of a seamless connection with the heroes of a Russian past and, as the dictator put it in 1945, fought the war to its bitter victory in a *union sacrée*, where Russians per force and by nature assumed the role of being the 'leading nation of all the nations belonging to the Soviet Union', the peoples' 'guiding force'.[35]

The Soviets and the Jews

Not long after, the post-war target of what has been labelled 'Stalin's last crime' became the USSR's Jews. 'Every Jew nationalist', the elderly dictator pronounced in December 1952, 'is an agent of American intelligence'.[36] Stalin's death three months later ended what may have been preparations for an 'ethnic' purge. How before that time had Jewish identity been squared with the Soviet state and its purpose?

Romanov Russia had been notorious for its anti-Semitism, framed less with the pseudo-science of the Nazis and more with a traditional religious and social hatred. Konstanin Pobedonostsev, tutor to Nicholas II and a man who tried to put the cause of reaction into words, had imagined, in a happy future, that 'a third of the Jews will be wiped out, a third will be converted, and a third will emigrate'. The various Marxist opponents of the existing regime before 1917 duly included many men and women of Jewish culture and, in July 1918, the Council of People's Commissars proclaimed its utter rejection of anti-Semitism: 'The anti-Semitic movement and the anti-Jewish pogroms are a deadly menace to the Revolution of the workers and peasants and [the Council] calls upon the workers in Socialist Russia to fight this plague with all possible means.'[37]

The USSR's pledged internationalism, in other words, seemed to suit no people better than it did those Jews who had not been convinced by Zionism to nationalize themselves and instead understood, in anti-Stalinist Marxist historian Isaac Deutscher's brilliant words: 'As Jews they dwelt on the borderlands of various civilizations, religions and national cultures. They were born and brought up on the borderlands of various epochs . . . Their minds lived on the margins or in the nooks and crannies of their respective nations.' Ethnically speaking, as well as in their intellectuality, they were 'non-Jewish Jews'.[38]

During the turmoil of the next two decades, the USSR's Jews fared relatively well. It was true that, during the 1920s, the leading Jewish Bolsheviks, Trotsky, Zinoviev and Kamenev, lost out

Isaac Deutscher

Isaac Deutscher was the independent Marxist biographer of Stalin and a historian who, until his death in Rome in 1967, stubbornly tried to resist the pull of the nation.

He was born in Cracow, then part of Austria-Hungary, in 1907. His father, Jacob, was a prosperous Jewish printer. Deutscher was a precocious child in a bookish household. By the age of 16, he was reading his poetry in public and had a book of poems published. His father meanwhile warned him against becoming too polonized since, he said, to discover civilization, you needed to go 'beyond Auschwitz' (a small town near Cracow).

In 1925 Deutscher moved to Warsaw in time for Poland's parliamentary regime to be overthrown by Marshal Pilsudski's militarist coup a year later. Deutscher joined the Polish Communist Party (illegal since 1919). From 1929 he was reading articles and pamphlets written by the exiled (from the USSR) Trotsky and other Marxist writings critical of Soviet developments. As a member of a Polish Communist delegation he visited the USSR in 1931 and, on his return, helped form an anti-Stalin opposition within the Party, resulting quickly in his expulsion from its ranks. By the late 1930s, already living in an increasingly anti-Semitic society, he had no doubt that Nazi Germany would soon expand into eastern Europe, and he decided to move west. He left Poland in April 1939.

When Deutscher emigrated, he was fluent in Polish, Yiddish, German and French but had no English. He settled in Britain in 1939 and, having joined up with the remnants of the defeated Polish army, he taught himself English at a camp in Scotland. He began writing articles on Soviet and eastern European affairs for English newspapers and soon became the regular contributor on these areas for *The Economist* (independent conservative) and *The Observer* (independent liberal).

After the war, he retired from journalism to concentrate on research for a massive history of the USSR. He found British publishers to be more interested in biography, and in 1946 he

was commissioned by Oxford University Press to write a
biography of Stalin, then at the height of his power and, outside
the USSR, notoriety. Deutscher, who, as he said, 'belonged to
those whom Stalin had cruelly defeated', began writing early in
1947 and finished late in 1948. *Stalin* (Oxford: Oxford University
Press) was published in 1949 and revised for republication in
1966–67. In a Cold War context, *Stalin* was attacked by both
Stalinists and anti-Stalinists, Cold War warriors and Trotskyites;
but it gave Deutscher global fame.

He moved on to a three-volume biography of Trotsky and
many further pamphlets and lectures, some in his capacity as
a philosopher of the 'new left'. To his death he remained
optimistic about the revolution. Once it shook off the legacy
of Stalin, he prophesied, it would create a happier and more
prosperous society than that functioning under capitalism.
Its internationalism, he was similarly sure, must one day
sweep away the petty rivalries and wars of the nations.

in Kremlin power struggles with Stalin and evident that the dictator from time to time mouthed populist anti-Semitic ideas.
Yet, for many, the USSR seemed a 'Jewish utopia . . . in power'.[39]
By contrast, continuing Zionist preaching of a national future
for the Jews as the summit of
happiness was dismissed as
wayward and mistaken. Internationalism, not nationalism,
solved the 'Jewish problem';
the USSR offered the best
model of modernity.

*Internationalism, not
nationalism, solved the
'Jewish problem'; the
USSR offered the best
model of modernity*

The statistics looked good, at least while the economic and
social inadequacies of the revolutionary state could be explained
away as temporary. During the New Economic Policy of the mid

1920s, the Jews did best of the Soviet peoples. Although comprising less than two per cent of the country's population, in Moscow Jews owned half or more of many types of store. After the New Economic Policy was abandoned and the Stalinist new course installed, Jewish prominence did not lessen. When in 1934 the Secret Police changed its name to the NKVD, Jews were the most numerous group among that body's leading cadres. In 1939, despite official efforts to favour the poor, Jews composed 17.1 per cent of university students in Moscow and 35.6 per cent in Kiev. In the USSR's most self-consciously sophisticated city, Leningrad, Jews constituted almost 70 per cent of dentists, 38.6 per cent of doctors, 31.3 per cent of writers of various kinds, and 18.4 per cent of university professors and scientists. 'Most members of the new [Stalinist] Soviet elite were not Jews, and most Jews were not members of the new Soviet elite. But there is no doubt that the Jews had a much higher proportion of elite members than any other ethnic group in the USSR.'[40] 'No other ethnic group', it has been remarked, 'was as good at being Soviet, and no other ethnic group was as keen on abandoning its language, rituals, and traditional areas of settlement.'[41] Jews were even underrepresented among those arrested in 1937–38 (about one per cent) and those in 1939 pent up in the gulag. 'Jews were the only large Soviet nationality without its own "native" territory that was not targeted for a purge during the Great Terror.'[42]

What is sometimes these days obscured is just how viciously Nazism attacked Marxists of all kinds and how tightly fused in Hitler's mind were the twin enemies of what he called 'Judaeo-Bolshevism'. The Soviet death toll after the Nazi invasion of the USSR is also somewhat forgotten; the fact that millions died as a result of the Soviet government's policies, even though the great majority fell to the Nazis, makes it hard to convert the Soviet story into a simple moral tale of willing executioners and innocent victims. Yet, in most ways, it was the Great Patriotic War that signalled the end of any credible pretence that the USSR could provide an internationalist solution to the dilemma of being Jewish.

The desperate war effort, with its massive casualties, reinforced the role of Russian nationalism in the Soviet amalgam, without ever fully installing it as the regime's ideology. Rather, the post-war USSR became a place where old Stalinist soldiers, administrators and commissars and their 'new' but really old culture from the 1930s never died and scarcely began to fade away until Gorbachev, and a new generation, finally emerged after 1985. As it fought the successive cold wars against the vastly wealthier and more flexible USA, the USSR ironically grew ever more frozen in its leading personnel, in its understanding of industrialization, in its framing of culture, in its coping with environmental degradation and in its unresolved dilemma about nationality. With its citizens still expected to mouth the words of the *Internationale* as communism's global anthem, the Soviet state strove uneasily to be a union of socialist republics, an ambition that seemed more and more lunatic in a world of nations.

The fate of the Jews in the first aftermath of the war and with the formation in 1948 of the state of Israel signalled another drastic turn in Soviet life. 'The ethnicization of the Soviet state and the nationalization of ethnic Jews . . . kept reinforcing each other'[43] until Stalin and officialdom discovered that Soviet Jews were a border people, very likely more menacing than those persecuted in the 1930s. Before that turning point, the regime and most Soviet Jews had been unsure whether they were an extra-territorial national minority, a religious community in an atheist state, an ethnic group on the brink of assimilation into Sovietism, or a nationality like the rest. But now the option to be a Marxist internationalist, a non-Jewish Jew, Soviet-style, became harder to sustain with every passing year. Between 1968 and 1982, 265 000 Soviet

> *The regime and most Soviet Jews had been unsure whether they were an extra-territorial national minority, a religious community in an atheist state, an ethnic group on the brink of assimilation into Sovietism, or a nationality like the rest*

Jews surmounted countless bureaucratic difficulties and emigrated, many to Israel,[44] with its national utopia excising any lingering belief in a Marxist cosmopolitan paradise. Still more were refused exit.

The late USSR and the nation

Meanwhile the USSR lurched on. Its leaders talked internationalism from time to time; Khrushchev, the peasant-born optimist and wide-eyed believer in technology, in 1961 placed on the Party Programme the prophecy that 'nations will draw together, until complete unity is achieved'. But his more cautious successors were more inclined to flirt with Russian nationalism and with anti-Semitism.[45] Alexander Solzhenitsyn, the dissident most celebrated in the west, expressed a more strident and soulful commitment to the Russian nation. In 1990, he happily favoured abandoning the outer reaches of empire. He simultaneously urged that 'all the talk of a separate Ukrainian people existing since something like the ninth century and possessing its own non-Russian language is a recently invented falsehood. We all sprang from precious Kiev', while also proclaiming that 'land' and contact to it, blood and soil, were what best expressed identity.[46]

When Gorbachev came to office, he still believed that the USSR was open to reform and must have thought that both socialism and internationalism retained an unharnessed potential and dynamism. One of his backers, the sometime dissident historian Roy Medvedev, certainly believed that, in the USSR, despite the squabbling that was scarring relations between the different republics, 'there was and there is cooperation among nations. There is a new historical and social community: the "Soviet people". All this is not a myth.'[47] Similarly, western historians lightly referred to the USSR as a nation; Geoffrey Hosking was only one among many when he asserted that the USSR was 'a nation traumatized by its own past'.[48]

The new Russia and the nation

In this comment, Hosking was right to emphasize that Gorbachev's greatest problem was the urgent need to grapple with history. In that regard, the rhythm of revision proved telling. First to be abandoned were Stalinism, the personality cult, collectivization, the purges and the rest of the gulag story. Next and much more slowly to be written off were Lenin and the revolution of 1917; maybe 'error' had crept in then, too. Still surviving when the USSR dissolved was the 'good' Second World War and its 'Russian' history. In Moscow, the rooms in the Museum of Contemporary History, dealing with the Great Patriotic War, remained dustily unchanged even in the 1990s.[49] The conflict, after all, could signify the sacrifice and triumph of the nation. It could thereby shrug off the defeat and liquidation of the USSR and its never wholly abandoned dreams of an international revolution and of a world that did not have to heave with the particular wishes and problems of each nation.

There have been plenty of wars of succession in the ex-USSR and rather more cases of the public preaching of crass nationalist ideas exceeding the norm in their foolishness, historical inaccuracy and potential to kill should anyone carry them into practice. The Russian 'Liberal Democrat' Vladimir Zhirinovsky, a politician lacking the remotest understanding of either liberty or democracy, in the 1990s could still 'dream of Russian soldiers washing their boots in the warm water of the Indian Ocean and wearing their summer uniform all the year round'.[50] The campaign against the Chechens, echoing Stalinist repression in the region during the Second World War and brutal Tsarist conquest a century earlier, continues.

Yugoslavia and the nation

Yet, for post-communist states, the epicentre of nationalist war and murder was Yugoslavia, or what soon became ex-Yugoslavia. The country was led until his death, aged 88, in May 1980 by Josef Broz, known as 'Tito', half Habsburg-style enlightened despot *redivivus*, half national communist dictator and anti-fascist resistance hero sprung from Yugoslavia's special and devastating Second World War. Under his rule, the communist state seemed, at least superficially, to be dealing with the national tensions that coursed through its seven constituent republics with aplomb.

As one western commentator remarked in 1976, Yugoslavia had become 'almost unrecognizable to those who knew the country a generation ago'.[51] Could Tito's realm be proving a smaller and more successful version of the internationalism promised but plainly not achieved in the USSR?

History, after all, did seem to offer lessons that it might be better to be a 'Yugoslav' than to pursue a Serb, Croat, Slovene, Macedonian, Bosnian, Montenegrin or Kosovan identity. Well before 1914, but especially in each of the wars, the area had been stained by ethnic massacres. Of all the combatant states in the First World War, Serbia suffered the highest casualty rate: the country lost 37.1 per cent of its mobilized men, a toll that amounted to more than a fifth of the male population aged between 15 and 49. This figure was five times the toll in Russia, almost four times that in Britain and twice that in Germany and France.[52] By 1917, 100 000 Serb soldiers were held in appalling conditions in Austrian concentration camps in the Balkans, while the occupying Austrians fostered Croat and Muslim militias, which engaged in the 'ethnic cleansing' and massacre of what were identified as Serb villages. On the other side, it has been estimated that at least 300 000 Croat soldiers died fighting in Habsburg armies.[53]

The Second World War was, if anything, worse, with the Yugoslav territory a prey to multiple civil and ideological wars. Even Joseph Goebbels grew squeamish at the behaviour of the fascist *Ustasha* state in independent Croatia, which he complained had instituted 'a regime of terror that defies description'.[54] The figures remain disputed but, during the war, more than a tenth of Yugoslavia's population perished, the majority at the hands of fellow countrymen. Then, with victory, the communist partisans executed 20 000 Serb nationalists (or cetniks), 10 000 Slovene 'Home Guard' 'collaborators', 5000 Bosnian Muslims (another ethnic group accepted into the Waffen SS) and perhaps 360 000 Croats.[55]

This dreadful legacy undoubtedly did weigh on post-1945 Yugoslavia. Yet, in great part in this society, 'the present explains the past'.[56] After all, the imposition of communist rule in postwar eastern Europe coincided with the culmination of the 'ethnic cleansing' that had disfigured many wartime states, except that now the greatest number of expellees, up to 15 million of them, were *Volksdeutsche*, ethnic Germans by one definition or another.[57] Every eastern European country became more ethnically coherent than it had been between the wars, when, as has been noted, ethnic division had so often prompted authoritarian rule. Some current historians want to spotlight the tragedy involved for individuals and families in these forced population transfers.[58] Yet, in a world of nations, perhaps some sort of rough justice was then achieved and the chances of a third world war waged by a Germany that was again revisionist were reduced.[59]

Although it, too, ruthlessly expelled its German and Italians subjects, the post-1945 country in the region that still lacked a dominant nationality was Yugoslavia. In the 1981 state census, 1.2 million out of 22.4 million identified themselves as 'Yugoslavs'. Even though Tito soon broke free of Soviet tutelage, and Yugoslavia became the 'border state' of the communist zone, much of the story of the USSR's ambiguous coping with the nationalities of all the Russias was now repeated. The Yugoslav constitution pledged national blindness. Yet it also recognized seven different republics and offered to defend 'minority rights' when threatened, while, at least theoretically, envisaging a right of secession for a disgruntled group.[60] In these contradictions lay the opportunity for the nations of Yugoslavia to reinvent themselves should events offer cynical politicians advantage in so doing.

A similar opening for the revival of a national sense sprang from Yugoslavia's failure to do anything to solve the gap between the richer republics, headed by Slovenia in the north, and the poorer ones in the south. Such regional difference was scarcely a Yugoslav problem alone. Across the Adriatic, Italy, in quite a few ways the border state of capitalism, was similarly finding its 'southern problem' never ending. But, in Yugoslavia, the collection of statistics illustrating difference and the associated fostering of moralism about why it occured, combined with the apparent evidence of present or historical 'injustice' or both, paved the way after Tito's death for the newly open nationalism. The defence of the nation became the cause of the Serb Party chief, Slobodan Milosevic, by origin a 'soft-spoken banker',[61] and of those thrusting themselves forward as national saviours in the other republics.

In sum, the Yugoslavia that collapsed in the 1990s offers another grim instance where nationalizers from above, evidently seeking personal gain somewhere in their rhetoric about the 'liberation' of their 'people', were able to evoke passion from below, and a commitment to national identity that was rapidly reinforced when terrible events separated erstwhile neighbours from each other. Hating, it seems, comes all but naturally. The Croat journalist Slavenka Drakulic, daughter of a family that had tried to be Yugoslav, has memorably remarked that 'once the concept of "otherness" takes root, the unimaginable becomes possible'.[62] It is equally true that once the unimaginable starts to happen, once people are or can view themselves as victims, the sense of 'otherness' spreads and becomes entrenched. Both in the USSR and in Yugoslavia, communism failed to provide its subjects with a level of economic or cultural ease that

The Yugoslavia that collapsed in the 1990s offers another grim instance where nationalizers from above were able to evoke passion from below, and a commitment to national identity that was rapidly reinforced when terrible events separated erstwhile neighbours from each other

might insulate them against nationalism. The challenge that Lenin's internationalism may have offered in 1918–19 to Wilson's self-determination had, throughout the history of communism, been unable to convince very many that it could offer a solution to the problem of human beings living together.

Yet, the wrecking of the Marxist view, however deluded, that a universalized working class could achieve the Enlightenment hope in a common humankind, spread contentedly across the globe, carried a cost. In its fall the USSR brought ruin to, or imposed a severe check on, all other internationalist solutions to the globe's political problems, a certainly odd and arguably terrifying situation just as economists and bankers seem convinced that 'globalization' is the best mechanism through which to make us universally richer and happier. Capitalism, we are assured, will multiply for ever the wealth of nations and, over

Maybe Adam Smith will prove no better than Karl Marx in sketching a resolution of the fondness men and women have to hate, destroy and kill and to use a process of national othering to justify their actions

the past two centuries, there is plenty of evidence that might prove the case. Yet, not far below the surface, the contradictions in a universally nationalized capitalism seem as glaring as those that did so much to destroy the global ambitions of communism. Maybe Adam Smith will prove no better than Karl Marx in sketching a resolution of the fondness men and women have to hate, destroy and kill and to use a process of national othering to justify their actions.

Notes

1   L. Trotsky, *1905* (1972, Harmondsworth: Penguin), p. 152.

2   I. Maisky, *Journey into the Past* (1962, London: Hutchinson), pp. 166–7. Kollontai, the daughter of a general, was then a libertarian and a feminist Bolshevik.

3   L. Trotsky, *Stalin: An Appraisal of the Man and his Influence* (1969, London: Panther), pp. 19–21.

4   A.J. Rieber, 'Stalin, man of the borderlands', *American Historical Review*, 2001, 106, pp. 1651–91.

5   For this still brilliant insight into Lenin, see E. Wilson, *To the Finland Station: A Study in the Writing and Acting of History* (1960, London: Fontana), pp. 375–406.

6   Trotsky, *Stalin*, p. 200.

7   S. Fitzpatrick, 'Cultural revolution as class war', in S. Fitzpatrick (ed.), *Cultural Revolution in Russia, 1928–1931* (1978, Bloomington, IN: Indiana University Press), p. 16.

8 R.C. Tucker, *Stalin as Revolutionary 1879–1929: A Study in History and Personality* (1974, London: Chatto and Windus), pp. 183–4.

9 Cited by Y. Slezkine, *Arctic Mirrors: Russia and the Small Peoples of the North* (1994, Ithaca, NY: Cornell University Press), p. 141.

10 I. Deutscher, *Stalin: A Political Biography* (1966, Harmondsworth: Penguin), p. 190.

11 Slezkine, *Arctic Mirrors*, p. 141.

12 R. Stites, *The Women's Liberation Movement in Russia: Feminism, Nihilism, and Bolshevism 1860–1930* (1990, Princeton, NJ: Princeton University Press), p. 366.

13 M. McAuley, *Bread and Justice: State and Society in Petrograd 1917–1922* (1991, Oxford: Clarendon), p. 5.

14 For background, see A.F. Upton, 'Finland', in S.J. Woolf (ed.), *European Fascism* (1968, London: Weidenfeld and Nicolson), pp. 184–216.

15 P.M. Austin, 'Soviet Karelian: the language that failed', *Slavic Review*, 1992, 51, p. 24.

16 G. Hosking, 'The Second World War and Russian national consciousness', *Past and Present*, 2002, 175, p. 165.

17 Austin, 'Soviet Karelian', p. 33.

18 Y. Slezkine, 'From savages to citizens: the cultural revolution in the Soviet Far North', *Slavic Review*, 1992, 51, p. 73.

19 Slezkine, *Arctic Mirrors*, p. 13.

20 Slezkine, 'From savages to citizens', p. 73.

21 *Ibid.* p. 76.

22 A. Wilson, *The Ukrainians: Unexpected Nation* (2000, New Haven, CT: Yale University Press), pp. 22–7, 38, 88.

23 *Ibid.* pp. 108–9.

24 I. Prizel, *National Identity and Foreign Policy: Nationalism and Leadership in Poland, Russia and Ukraine* (1998, Cambridge: Cambridge University Press), pp. 162–3.

25 Wilson, *The Ukrainians*, pp. 129–133.

26 G.O. Liber, *Soviet Nationality Policy, Urban Growth and Identity Change in the Ukrainian SSR 1923–1934* (1992, Cambridge: Cambridge University Press), pp. 69, 147.

27 C. Wanner, *Burden of Dreams: History and Identity in Post-Soviet Ukraine* (1998, University Park, PA: Pennsylvania State University Press), p. 17.

28 Liber, *Soviet Nationality Policy*, pp. 91, 168.

29 Wanner, *Burden of Dreams*, p. 150.

30 A. Weiner, 'Nature, nurture, and memory in a socialist utopia: delineating the Soviet socio-ethnic body in the age of socialism', *American Historical Review*, 1999, 1904, p. 1137.

31 A. Weiner, *Making Sense of War: The Second World War and the Fate of the Bolshevik Revolution* (2001, Princeton, NJ: Princeton University Press), pp. 20–23, 160.

32 F. Hirsch, 'The Soviet Union as a work-in-progress: ethnographers and the category *nationality* in the 1926, 1937, and 1939 censuses', *Slavic Review*, 1997, 56, pp. 255–6.

33 D. Shearer, 'Elements near and alien: passportization, policing, and identity in the Stalinist State, 1932–1952', *Journal of Modern History*, 2004, 76, pp. 839, 846.

34 T. Martin, 'The origins of Soviet ethnic cleansing', *Journal of Modern History*, 1998, 70, pp. 815–16, 830, 855.

35 J. Barber and M. Harrison, *The Soviet Home Front, 1941–1945: A Social and Economic History of the U.S.S.R. in World War II* (1991, London: Longman), pp. 113, 115–16.

36 J. Brent and V.P. Naumov, *Stalin's Crime: The Doctors' Plot* (2003, London: John Murray), p. 270.

37 K. Pinkus, *The Jews of the Soviet Union: The History of a National Minority* (1988, Cambridge: Cambridge University Press), pp. 23, 85.

38 I. Deutscher, *The Non-Jewish Jew and other Essays* (1981, London: Merlin Press), p. 27.

39 Y. Slezkine, *The Jewish Century* (2004, Princeton, NJ: Princeton University Press), p. 216.

40 *Ibid.* pp. 218–19, 221, 223–4, 236.

41 *Ibid.* p. 247.

42 *Ibid.* pp. 273–4.

43 *Ibid.* p. 297.

44 Pinkus, *The Jews of the Soviet Union*, pp. 57, 305.

45 Prizel, *National Identity and Foreign Policy*, pp. 191–5.

46 A. Solzhenitsyn, *Rebuilding Russia: Reflections and Tentative Proposals* (1991, London: Harvill), pp. 17, 30.

47 R. Medvedev and G. Chiesa, *Time of Change: An Insider's View of Russia's Transformation* (1989, New York: Pantheon), p. 214.

48 G. Hosking, *The Awakening of the Soviet Union* (1990, Cambridge MA: Mandarin), p. 8.

49 C. Merridale, 'Redesigning history in contemporary Russia', *Journal of Contemporary History*, 2003, 38, p. 17.

50 S.P. Talbott, 'Vladimir Zhirinovsky and the December 1993 elections: current prospects for fascism in Russia', *Slovo*, 1995, 8, p. 74. Zhirinovsky added that the Russians might have to deal with their minorities as 'America did with the Indians and the Germans with the Jews . . . I may have to shoot 100 000 people, but the other 300 million will live peacefully.'

51 F. Singleton, *Twentieth-Century Yugoslavia* (1976, London: Macmillan), p. 305.

52 N. Ferguson, *The Pity of War* (1998, London: Penguin), p. 299.

53 J.R. Lampe, *Yugoslavia as History: Twice there was a Country*
    (1996, Cambridge: Cambridge University Press), pp. 105–6.

54 J. Goebbels, *Final Entries 1945: Diaries* (ed. H. Trevor-Roper)
    (1978, New York: Putnam's), p. 61.

55 Lampe, *Yugoslavia as History*, p. 224; S.P. Ramet, *Balkan Babel: The
    Disintegration of Yugoslavia from the Death of Tito to the War for Kosovo*
    (1999, Boulder, CO: Westview Press), p. 4.

56 J.B. Allcock, *Explaining Yugoslavia* (2000, London: Hurst), p. 349.

57 For a maximum figure, see T. Judt, 'The past is another country:
    myth and memory in post-war Europe', in J.W. Müller (ed.), *Memory
    and Power in Postwar Europe: Studies in the Presence of the Past* (2002,
    Cambridge: Cambridge University Press), p. 162.

58 *Ibid.* p. 163.

59 See this conclusion at the start of the 1960s in J.B. Schechtman,
    Postwar Population Transfers in Europe 1945–1955 (1962, Philadelphia,
    PA: University of Pennsylvania Press), pp. 374–5.

60 A. Djilas, *The Contested Country: Yugoslav Unity and Communist
    Revolution, 1919–1953* (1991, Cambridge, MA: Harvard University
    Press), pp. 160–68.

61 Ramet, *Balkan Babel*, p. 6.

62 S. Drakulic, *The Balkan Express: Fragments from the Other Side of the
    War* (1994, New York: Harper), p. 3.

CHAPTER 6

Minorities old and new, and the nation since 1945

THE DEFEAT OF NAZI-FASCISM in 1945 and that of communism at the beginning of the 1990s seemed proof that history could only go one way. Communists had stupidly sought a false equality and their internationalism had proven a sad joke. Nazifascists had perverted the positive sense of national belonging into war, xenophobia and racial massacre; their obsession with 'enemies within' defined in ethnic terms and justified by pseudoscience had matched the Soviets' fanatical determination to reward the working class and liquidate the rest. Both ideologies were 'totalitarian'. They were, therefore, evil. But they had also lost. Their time was past. Now everyone could enjoy a new world order, composed through a fusion of the nation, the market and freedom. Despite the hint of contradiction involved, the formula half sketched in 1848 and given firmer line by Woodrow Wilson in 1919 seemed to have won universal and permanent victory.

Globalization and its discontents

Capitalism had long reckoned uneasily with being confined into the variously sized and unevenly 'developed' nations, so tousled by destructive wars, petty economic rivalry and self-interested legislation designed, it was said, to bring short-term benefit to cynical politicians and greedy pressure groups

Already in the 1980s, the world was beginning to hear in an emphatic tone that its future lay in 'globalization'. Capitalism had long reckoned uneasily with being confined into the variously sized and unevenly 'developed' nations, so tousled by destructive wars, petty economic rivalry and self-interested legislation designed, it was said, to bring short-term benefit to cynical politicians and greedy pressure groups. Under the impulse of such leaders as Margaret Thatcher in the UK and Ronald Reagan in the USA, the world could abandon the fiscal inefficiency of the over-bureaucratized welfare state. Now, at last, the market could have full rein. Adroit bankers could purge the system of any momentary glitches. The resulting free trade would bring wealth to all nations and individuals.

In this regard, one matter increasingly thrust itself forward as nations pushed ahead with 'reform'. Among the commerce needing greater liberalization, globalizers maintained at first cheerfully, was that in peoples. The market decreed that every nation state should allow immigration or emigration as the flows of employment and the demand for skills required. In this regard, twenty-first-century globalizing capitalism should transcend the nation both in its international dealings and domestically as it directed new citizens, people with different histories, languages, cultures and belief systems, into every 'developed' nation state. Some time in a better future, the promise was, every nation would be multicultural, places not of cruel totalitarian homogeneity but of richly infinite variety, yet somehow also united.

Twenty years after the initial political triumphs of the globalizers, the record of their achievement remains uneven. Statistics record economic growth for many parts of the developed world and an even greater advance for the various states of 'Asia', be they communist, if scarcely Marxist, China, half socialist or communalist India, and capitalist but corporatist Korea and Japan. Along with these successes, however, have come failures – war and massacre in the Middle East; war, massacre, 'tribalism', disease and famine in Africa; and, in curious accompaniment, pervasive and even paranoid fear in the developed world about 'terrorism', 'fundamentalism' and 'aliens'. 'Enemies within' are back in business. Whereas, during the unhappy era between the wars, states moved to eliminate those who did not fit the national spirit or bloodstocks, now countries worry about the importation through their immigrants of foreign and fundamentalist fanaticisms. In the first decade of the twenty-first century, everywhere politicians have begun to curtail the cultural largesse of multiculturalism; everywhere, with the assistance of the stridently nationalist (if global) Murdoch press, citizens have narrowed their empathy about human suffering and nationalized themselves with a rigour that belied the utopian hopes of liberal globalization. Now 'national values' are what matter; humane values and the other hopes of the Enlightenment are becoming irrelevant.

The epicentre of these developments lies in a new and potentially permanent war, a battle directed against a nebulous but seemingly global 'terror'. The terrorists, it is maintained, will stop at nothing to impose their mad will

The epicentre of these developments lies in a new and potentially permanent war, a battle directed against a nebulous but seemingly global 'terror'. The terrorists, it is maintained, will stop at nothing to impose their mad will. In return the nation states should stop at little in fighting them. Collateral damage (for which read 'civilian massacre') and the targeted elimination of fanatics (for which read 'unapologetic assassination and murder') became daily events, scarcely in need of explanation or justification. 'Freedom' might be the ultimate good but, our ruling elites argue, for the present it needs to be controlled, circumscribed and policed with greater rigour. Immigrants and refugees may transmogrify in time into deserving settlers or useful workers in the more prosperous states but, during the process of their 'assimilation' or 'integration', their behaviour and attitudes need careful watching. Those who fail the national test should be jailed or expelled or both.

As the new millennium unfolds, globalization may be the only economic alternative, but our world presently seems more determinedly divided into warring societies than it was when the Cold War overrode national borders and concentrated conflict into a fight between communists and their foes

In sum, as the new millennium unfolds, globalization may be the only economic alternative, but our world presently seems more determinedly divided into warring societies than it was when the Cold War overrode national borders and concentrated conflict into a fight between communists and their foes. The more we globalize, the more we need to nationalize, and the public ceremonies and fanfare, and the private lies, of the nation must hide the common powerlessness of national politicians to oppose global economic forces.

How has this situation arisen? What was the effect of the spread of nation states beyond the European source of the national idea? How have new nations dealt with the dilemma of their novelty when the nation anxiously wants to proclaim its ancient birth? What, too, have societies, both old and new, made of immigration, with its constant importation of new histories and new ways of relating past, present and future into nations proclaiming that they arm their citizens with a permanent mastery over time? Furthermore, how have national assertions about eternity coped with the pretensions of ancient religions to resolve the meaning of birth, life and death by telling old, old stories and by awarding a god or gods powers beyond the rational?

The case of Australia

In attempting to answer these questions the appropriate place to begin is my own nation of birth, citizenship and home. Australia is not normally viewed as a country beset by history and yet presently it, too, is a site of the hopes and dilemmas of globalized capitalism endeavouring to coexist with a narrowing nationalized culture and ethic. In contemporary Australia it is hard to think of any aspect of life that is not habitually nationalized. Every activity is judged through its alleged embodying of

'Australian values'. This verbal primacy attributed to the nation has occurred despite the apparent novelty of Australia's political past (white settlers first made landfall in what was not yet Australia in 1788), the derivativeness of much of local culture, inevitably conditioned by the power of the USA and by Australians' usage of the world-ranging English language, and a scepticism towards rhetorical excess once treasured by Australians as something of an identifying feature. When, in the 1960s, the comparative study of 'new societies' (as they were innocently labelled) was historiographically fashionable, Australia was deemed to 'enshrine' the 'radical conservatism of the Chartists [in Britain] and of [William] Cobbett'.[1] The country, the American liberal Louis Hartz maintained, was the nation where the 'Labor spirit' had effortlessly conquered.[2] Australia, a younger colleague of his concluded, could best be understood as the centre of 'socialist *laissez-faire*', 'New Lanark writ large'.[3] Australian nationalism, he acknowledged, was a powerful and even pervasive force, but it remained structurally egalitarian and was typically expressed without bragging or excess. National commonsense comprehended that those who favoured social democracy were genuine Australians and those who opposed it were not, and left patriotic rodomontade to others.[4]

In framing their conclusions about Antipodean national identity, these American commentators acknowledged a debt to the 'Bush legend' of the Australian radical historian Russel Ward, an advocate of the idea that the staunchly egalitarian Australian man (he paid scant attention to women) was forged by the need for mateship with his fellows in developing the outback.[5] In so arguing, Ward was seeking to overturn the conclusions of the more decorous Sir Keith Hancock, who, back in the 1930s, had depicted Australians as '98 per cent British' and, delighted to be so, 'independent Australian Britons'. For these 'transplanted' people, Hancock advised, 'pride of race' counted for more than 'love of country'. As a result, Australians hated glib parallels between themselves and the USA, while being ferociously deter- mined to remain a 'white' country. The legislation banning any immigration from Asia, Hancock and, in his view, his fellow Australians applauded, as 'the indispensable condition of every Australian policy'.[6]

Although Australia's leading Cold War politician Sir Robert Menzies constructed his persona around being a 'Queen's man', the Second World War brought changes to Australians' fate as it did to many peoples. After victory in the Pacific, immigration policy jumped track. With Britons unwilling to come to a far-off country, which had learned from its brief experience of Japanese bombing that it needed to 'populate or perish', first what were called (in naive mimicking of the racial theoretics propounded by the Nazis) 'northern Europeans', then 'eastern Europeans' and finally 'southern Europeans' were let in. During the 1950s, the largest groups of newcomers were either Italian or Greek. When the Mediterranean states grew too wealthy to foster overseas emigration, the pendulum of acceptability swung further east, by the 1970s allowing 'Vietnamese' (often, in practice, minority Chinese from that country) to become immigrants. Then, at long last, the 'White Australia Policy' was abandoned and Australian politicians of both left and right began to evince enthusiasm about the country being 'multicultural'. Immigration had been thought too serious, and too potentially divisive, a matter not to be approached by the parties except in a bipartisan manner. Al Grassby, a flamboyant Labor Party minister of immigration

(1972–74), cheerfully proclaimed that 'we are all ethnics now'; 'the major task confronting Australia', he contended, 'is not to decide whether or not we have a multi-cultural society. We *have* a multi-cultural society. The first challenge is to make it work.'[7]

There were three key features of this new style Australian nation now being manufactured. The first was the endorsement of multiculturalism and so the approving of a political entity called Australia, which yet contained many histories, ranging from those of the various indigenous groups who had greeted white settlement in 1788 through the erstwhile mainstream ones of British and Irish Australia, and on to the complex of pasts imported with every migrant 'community' or with every individual migrant. Multiculturalism seemed to promise a nation that would be simultaneously one and many.

The idea of a country generously rich in histories and designedly loose in its mental borders did not establish itself. Where nationalism was concerned, the one could not tolerate an ostensible privileging of the many for long

Yet the idea of a country generously rich in histories and designedly loose in its mental borders did not establish itself. Where nationalism was concerned, the one could not tolerate an ostensible privileging of the many for long. For most of those engaged in forging the nation, multiculturalism meant little more than a public celebration of immigrant dance and cuisine. In any arena where power operated, it had to bow to the homogenizing purpose of the nation. Migrant 'communities', as they were now habitually labelled, were after all products of a nationalizing process, too, where, as an Italian commentator had mused many years earlier, on leaving a home-land: 'We discovered in ourselves for the first time our country and its stamp.'[8] Each ethnic community became a mini-nation, with a (self-promoted) leadership, with icons and symbols, and with an attempt to seize the historical high ground for itself and thereby fob off challenges from others. A competition soon broke out among 'community historians' to locate hidden 'ethnics' on the First or Second Fleets of white settlement, while Antonio Giordano, a 'community' leader in South Australia, reckoned that Marco Polo could have seen the western coast of the continent during his journeys. The Venetian traveller, he argued, could thereby be elevated to the rank of 'Father of Italo-Australia'.[9]

In a process that was scarcely confined to Australia but was replicated in all developed-world recipients of immigrants, multiculturalism rapidly dwindled into the most superficial aspect of those 'identity politics' that, from the 1970s, were every-where ousting class struggle from its century-old pre-eminence. In Australia, at least as influential as ethnic groups were the women's movement and those who preached the cause of what were now regularly, if anachronistically, called the 'first Australians', that is, the descendants of those 'Aboriginals' who had survived the irruption into their lands of European settlers. Engaged in working the themes of 'race' and 'gender' into the national past were a busy school of leftist historians, led initially by the grand, if antique, figure of Manning Clark. He was replaced from the 1980s by more humdrum successors, anxious to confront the past but still proud of the nation and hopeful about its future, being in other words the heirs and successors of the earlier radical tradition.

Manning Clark

In 1962, the first book appeared of what eventually was to be a seven-volume *History of Australia*. Its author was a professor at the Australian National University (ANU) in Canberra, C.M.H. ('Manning') Clark.

Clark had been born in Melbourne in 1915, son of a poorish clergyman father and a mother whose family came from the landed elite. After school and university education in his home city, he went to Oxford in 1938, reaching Europe in time to view the successes of Nazism there. He happened to arrive in Bonn in the immediate aftermath of the pogrom known as *'Krystallnacht'*. It was, he remarked characteristically, 'a great darkness'. A postgraduate study of De Tocqueville did not proceed far and Clark felt out of place in the UK (the Oxford cricket team dropped him for a local and statistically inferior wicket-keeper who had, however, been to an English public school).

In late 1940, Manning Clark returned to Australia to teach at the elite and private boys' school Geelong Grammar. He soon moved to Melbourne University and the ANU, then in its infancy, where in 1949 he became and remained professor. His hope, he reiterated on many occasions, was to view the human condition with 'the eye of pity' and 'to be there when everyone suddenly understands what it has been for'. He died in 1991.

Increasingly, his *History*, other writings and public commentaries elevated him to a national celebrity, loved by many on the Labor left and hated by the right (there was an absurd posthumous attempt in the Murdoch press to damn him as a Soviet agent of influence; Clark had published in 1960 a thin but by no means stupid account, *Meeting Soviet Man*, of a visit he made to the USSR in 1958). Clark's fame was occasioned by the conjoining of his historical endeavours with the enhanced nationalism that bubbled to the surface in 1970s Australia and still marks both left and right of the political pendulum.

Whereas his 'dryasdust' predecessors and those who succeeded him generally were mild-mannered in their themes and their writing, Clark approached the national past in the grand manner. He is best understood as a Michelet, curiously adapted to the late twentieth century. The characters of his story habitually wrestle with the profound or unspeakable – few other contemporary historians were as willing as Clark to locate 'dionysian frenzies' in the Antipodes. Clark's language owed a heavy debt to the King James Bible and Book of Common Prayer and he loved to quote the tortured and pessimistic Russian nationalist Fyodor Dostoevesky (no Bolshevik, he).

Clark's first volume opened with the claim that 'civilization did not begin in Australia until the last quarter of the eighteenth century' (a phrase later to be explained away when Aboriginal history was nationalized). Clark's theme remained that Australia was unique as a nation constructed purely in the aftermath of the Enlightenment and, in its best moments, sought the high ideals of liberty, equality and fraternity (women's issues appeared belatedly in his prose). Increasingly his version of the national history turned into a battle between a noble people (best expressed politically in the Labor Party) and a wodge of blinkered rich, men given to 'grovelling' to Britain and 'measuring' the world soullessly in their own short-term, selfish and rapacious interest. Clark, in sum, was an inventor of the nation, if one who feared that national unity and good were not yet achieved

It was true that the independent Sydney historian Richard White had cautioned in 1981 (and so before Hobsbawm) that 'there is no "real" Australia waiting to be uncovered'. The idea of the nation was a European importation, thus ensuring that 'each addition to the Australian identity has reflected changing intellectual needs and fashions in the West'. Kipling and Charles Darwin had contributed more to it than had any local author.[10] But such analysis did not stem the enthusiasm with which Australians of many different ideological stances greeted the

idea that history and all other cultural pursuits should be nationalized. The expansion of national time achieved by blending a
'timeless' 'Aboriginal history' before 1788 into the national past
encouraged a slew of writers, film-makers and the rest to urge
that the roots of each Australian's identity lay in the soil. The
nation's best culturalist historian, Inga Clendinnen, concluded a
study of initial contact between what, with sublime anachronism,
she called the 'British' (the newcomers) and the 'Australians'
(the native peoples) in phrases that managed to be portentous
and cosy at the same time:

There remains a final mystery. Despite our long alienation, despite our
merely adjacent histories, and through processes I do not yet understand,
we are now more like each other than we are like any other people.
We even share something of the same style of humour, which is a subtle
but far-reaching affinity. Here, in this place, I think we are all
Australians now.[11]

Any scepticism towards such sentiments and the dewy nationalization that it preached began to carry the danger that its
advocate might seem 'racist'. Almost as bad was the idea that a
critic was a bearer of the deplorable 'cultural cringe', allegedly
indulged in by those who thought of themselves as independently participating in the intellectual debates of London, Paris
and New York.

While the left dallied with a nationalism founded in the
spirituality of Australian nature, local conservatives, anxious to
sweep to victory in Australia's 'history wars', were willing with
new aggression to pursue restrictionist immigration policies and
endorse assimilationist attitudes to immigrants that were once
decorously restrained by bipartisanship. The crucial spur to this

new assertiveness was a break-away populist movement led by Pauline Hanson (1954–), a sassy fish-and-chip-shop owner from a Queensland country town. In 1996, Hanson, despite her expulsion from the con-servative ('Liberal') party, won election to the House of Rep-resentatives in Canberra and there used a maiden speech to attack both 'Asian immigra-tion' and welfare for Abori-ginals. In 1997, she founded a movement called One Nation, promising national unity and homogeneity. Her candidates

While the left dallied with a nationalism founded in the spirituality of Australian nature, local conservatives, anxious to sweep to victory in Australia's 'history wars', were willing with new aggression to pursue restrictionist immigration policies and endorse assimilationist attitudes to immigrants that were once decorously restrained by bipartisanship

briefly prospered in a succession of Australian state elections, polling more than 20 per cent in some places.

Like other Poujadist-style rightist populists, however, mem-bers of the movement lacked internal discipline and cohesion. One Nation was a movement of many competing factions, and Hanson these days is selling real estate. Her 'failure', however, was not only self-induced, since the neo-conservative Australian prime minister John Howard, in office from 1996 with a global-izing economic programme expanding on the 'reform' already introduced by his Labor predecessors, had in the 1980s flirted with the terminology and targets of One Nation. After his acces-sion to power, Howard moved with considerable political skill to emasculate Hanson's followers, winning to his cause people who were the most obvious losers in 'reform' and now known as 'Howard's battlers'.

The intellectual and ideological deception practised on such people has been cloaked by a great expansion in a conservative Australian nationalism. In the new millennium, Australians are reminded daily by the Murdoch and other conservative press of 'their' great sportsmen and sportswomen, 'their' military prowess (the Australian cricket team has taken to steeling itself by visits to Gallipoli in Turkey, where Anzac – Australian and New Zealander – troops fought under allegedly incompetent British command in 1915), 'their' steady mastering of the environment as commenced by heroic 'pioneers' and the sacrifice more recently made by 'their' 'victims of terror'. Those who lost their lives in Bali and Jakarta and on 11 September 2001 had their suffering automatically nationalized and directed at winning the nation a place on the podium in the Olympic Games of victimhood (and so countering the leftist nationalists' view that Aboriginals were those who had been subjected to an Australian holocaust).

The nation continent whose population has only just surpassed 20 million, a country that boasts an expanding economy, still welcomes quite a number of immigrants. But these days the official line is that assimilation is what is expected of these newcomers. Unity is the key. In a menacing world, only 'Australian values' can carry the nation through to greater glory and increased prosperity. In an Australia warring against terror, the immigrants' stories can only linger, in so far as they

> *These days the official line is that assimilation is what is expected of these newcomers*

can be nationalized, as part of the fruitful 'contribution' of all settlers to 'one Australia'.

Multiculturalism for all

The Australian situation and the language that expressed it are scarcely unique. In 1969, Pope Paul VI, in an encyclical entitled *'Pastoralis Migratorum Cura'* ('On the pastoral care of migrants'), sketched a universal multiculturalism as he preached that migration was 'proof of a love that surpasses borders' and called for a 'new humanitarianism' in protecting and approving migrant cultures.[12] First Canada and then the various European states, as their economies required fresh workers (some, such as Italy, moving with astonishing rapidity from being emigrant to immigrant countries in a few years of 'economic miracle'), uneasily developed a political stance on the 'absorption' of aliens. The fact that, in Britain and France especially, the majority of immigrants came from the nation's decolonized empire rendered the definition of their foreignness, and just what might be licit and what illicit in it for the nation, a complex matter provoking political dispute. Other European states, with Germany the model, sought to have the best of both worlds by treating immigrants as 'guest workers', people who could perform the dirty tasks at the bottom of the capitalist heap from one generation to the next but without acquiring citizenship and so perpetually vulnerable to eventual expulsion, should the economic need for them vanish.

In sum, in the developed world, immigration has become the most contested aspect of national life. Once, nineteenth-century manufacturers of nationhood were used to smoothing the track from the past so that it could tell a national tale and that only.

They did so at peril to those minorities most difficult to fold into the nation. But, with the globalization of migration (numerous 'refugees' complicated the matter further), aliens kept arriving from abroad and constantly countermanded cheap talk about national uniformity and unanimity. Once again the nationalist pretension to frame eternity for the people was under threat.

The case of the USA

The real model of a new-world nation, built by immigrants and always willing to accept more of them to turn the wheels of its marvellous capitalist economy, was the only genuine super power of the post-1945 era, the USA

But the real model of a new-world nation, built by immigrants and always willing to accept more of them to turn the wheels of its marvellous capitalist economy, was the only genuine super power of the post-1945 era, the USA. How had that nation conceptualized the place of new settlers and were there changes in that conceptualization after the Second World War?

When Louis Hartz was thinking comparatively about 'new societies', his USA had been constituted through the liberal and rational ideals of John Locke and the English Revolution of 1688.[13] In Hartz's view, the USA effortlessly combined a muted but powerful sense of nationality with a visceral dedication to liberalism, in both the political and economic worlds. For Hartz, the USA was a natural democracy in much the same way that the current rhetoric of George W. Bush and his aides assumes it to be. All were certain that a commitment to the nation and to its liberties, as expressed, for example, in the daily school ceremonies of saluting the flag, was 'banal' in the good sense of the word.[14] Above other peoples, Americans had imagined a genuine community. 'Nation building' in the USA was pervasive, continuous, ordinary and accepted by all. Being American was as American as apple pie.

Other interpretations were and are possible. Even after its own 'glorious revolution' and its proclamation that it stood for a new order where all men were created equal, the USA retained slavery. With the Yankee victory in the American Civil War, the American government overthrew legal slavery in the Emancipation Proclamation of 1863 and the Civil Rights Act of 1866, but the aftermath of this liberation by no means ensured that blacks rose to the level of whites, whether the index involved was legal or practical. Not even war service guaranteed full equality. Rather, during the Second World War, black people in the US army still served as 'second-class soldiers', and their treatment left major questions as to whether that conflict could really be deemed the 'Good War'. 'As in 1917, black servicemen were almost exclusively in labor battalions: loading ships, cleaning up, kitchen work, digging one thing or another. They were domestics abroad as well as at home.' Although, per force some eventually served at the front, the mythology held that 'blacks were not to be trusted in combat' for the nation.[15]

The battles in the Pacific were similarly fought with special racial animus, given that the majority of Americans were certain that the Japanese were racially alien and inferior. A liberal historian, writing in 1946, underlined that 'probably in all our history no foe has been so detested as were the Japs'.[16] For Americans in 1945, then, national and racial identities were hard to separate in importance and white, black and other coloured Americans had many reasons to draw different lessons and meanings from the nation.

For a brief moment after the war there was a reduction in immigration numbers. The thrusting nature of American capitalism, however, as well as the country's huge prosperity, soon saw immigrants again flocking in. They have continued to arrive: about one in nine of contemporary Americans is foreign-born.[17] Nonetheless, the 1970s brought something of a crisis in national identity. *Roots*, an evocatively titled book published in 1976 and a television series first screened in January 1977,[18] focused new public attention on the inequality so long endured by African Americans (as they were now to be called) and demanded an end to the silence about such issues in national history. The themes of *Roots* chimed with a view of the past that gave recognition, for the first time, to the African origins of this sector of the country and partially endorsed talk by radicals about 'black nationalism', separate from the mainstream. As early as 1961, one commentator had argued in words familiar in other nationalist discourse:

The tragedy of the Negro in America is that he has rejected his origins – the essentially human meaning in the history of slavery, prolonged suffering and social rejection. By rejecting this unique group experience and favoring assimilation and even biological amalgamation, he thus denies himself the creative possibilities inherent in it and in his folk culture. This 'dilemma' is fundamental; it severely limits his ability to evolve a new identity or a meaningful synthesis, capable of endowing his life with meaning and purpose.[19]

For quite a few in the leadership of the 'black community', winning a past needed to be harnessed to present action; now there was talk of 'black power' and separate development.

But African Americans were not the only segment of society deploying such words. During the liberal presidency of Jimmy Carter (1977–81), American multiculturalism and the idea that each immigrant 'community' was possessed of its own admirable and special history and, simultaneously, must mourn and mark its own time of suffering and victimhood, flowered. Conservatives began to worry that the country had become fissiparous and that the tolerance of too many community histories was hastening the decline of American power. By April 1975, the military and cultural defeat in Vietnam apparently settled the matter. Pundit Norman Glazer, a radical turned neo-conservative of Jewish background (born in New York in 1923), feared 'an increasing consciousness of the significance of group membership, an increasing divisiveness on the basis of race, color, and national origin, and a [resultant] spreading resentment among the disfavoured groups against the favored groups' was endangering the beneficent traditions of American democracy.[20]

Such pessimism proved misdirected. The USA had many evident strengths and was soon marching to victory in the Cold War. Massive numbers throughout the world continued to believe in the supreme virtue of an America that combined liberal political freedoms with the opportunity to shop. Any creases in American smiles were removed through a cheering popular and populist culture, well tailored to the superficial side of immigrant linguistic and social knowledge

Massive numbers throughout the world continued to believe in the supreme virtue of an America that combined liberal political freedoms with the opportunity to shop

and best reflected in Hollywood, that 'tinsel town' where the image banished all sadness and discontent, that 'dream factory' whose products were realer than real.

As if in proof that new settlers converted themselves to Americans first and foremost, among the key players in Hollywood were many people of immigrant stock, Italians, in most recent times African Americans, and Jews. By the fifth centenary in 1992 of Columbus's voyage, Italian-Americans may have been anxious to celebrate Columbus Day as theirs (and not share it with 'Hispanics', let alone with those who began to complain that the heroic voyager was a cruel and murderous invader) and so indulge in nationalization as people with 'Italian heritage'. Their historians even got around to arguing that, through internment, they had been victims in the US version of the Second World War. Yet, although community leaders might keep a weather eye on politics in Italy and help fund and favour the anti-communist cause there, by 1940 Italian-Americans had, in most senses, cut themselves off from their old country. They were now Italian-Americans with the stress on the second and not the first word, and with the hyphen to be included. In the USA they might celebrate the prettier, tastier and least offensive aspects of what could be painted as Italian national 'heritage'. But they were not anxious to situate their full identity in the Mediterranean.

The case of Jewish America

As so often in the history and historiography of the nation, the position for Jews was more complicated. Jewish migrants had been entering the USA for decades, flocking in from many different societies. In parallel with other 'alien' immigrants, they met quite a deal of prejudice; after 1933, the USA, like other potential host societies, allowed only a trickle of refugees to claim sanctuary on their shores, despite the deepening evidence of the murderousness of anti-Semitism in Germany and in states dominated by its fascist friends and allies. Nor after the war were American legislators at first enthusiastic about offering refuge to those who had survived the Nazi Judaeocide.

Nonetheless, 100 000 or more did gain entry to the USA. They joined the earlier settlers and were soon joyously accepting integration into an American nation where anti-Semitism was vanishing. Historian Peter Novick has explained that 'as an increasing number of Americans came to think of Jews as not significantly different from other Americans, an increasing number of American Jews came to think of themselves in the same way'.[21] They were people of a Jewish heritage that might or might not emphasize religious belief or instead treasure a more general culture. But their nationality was American and their politics democratic. They, too, were banal Americans.

A particularity in the story of many American Jews deepened, however, as they began to privilege what was, from the 1960s, coming to be called the Holocaust as a unique tragedy, an event wherein Jews suffered an incomparable victimhood. The Six Day War of 1967 and the more near-run Yom Kippur conflict of 1973 suggested that the appalling history of the 1930s and 1940s was about to repeat itself. 'The Holocaust, for many, was suddenly transformed from "mere", albeit tragic, history to imminent and terrifying prospect.'[22] Now the fate of Israel became hard to separate from the lives of the majority of American Jews, whatever their views about Zionism.

There was more than one corollary to this development. For America's Jews, despite their general prosperity – arguably they were 'by far the wealthiest, best-educated, most influential, in every way most successful group in American society'[23] – life in the USA became and remained edgy. 'Now there was an inward turn, an insistence on the defense of separate Jewish interests, a stress on what made Jews unlike other Americans',[24] and a fearfulness, a nagging suspicion that Jews were endangered there as everywhere else. The first aim of identity became to 'survive', while integration was regarded as the equivalent of self-immolation.[25] Helping survival was the possibility that past suffering could be alleviated by public apology, didactic commemoration and monetary recompense.

Holocausts for all

As has already been noted, the success of what is sometimes cynically labelled 'Shoah business' broadened into all 'identity politics', with every ethnic group seeking to imitate, if not match, the achievement of the 'Jewish community' (as, despite its manifest and multiple democratic divisions, it was being called) and to enhance their present profile through focus on some past suffering. In a curious inversion of fears about anti-Semitism, many immigrants began to think of themselves as 'all Jews now', at least in their determination that exploitation or worse in the past needed present amendment and reparation.

At the heights of American politics and culture, the sense of the nation and its position in the world also grew tenser. No sooner was the Cold War won than political scientist Samuel Huntington was prophesying that another, greater, conflict lay ahead in a grandiose battle between 'civilizations', especially one to be fought against 'Muslim fundamentalists'.[26] By 2004, Huntington was sure that the war against terror required further limitations in the banal liberalism of the American nation. 'Sub-national groups', he complained, should not be fostered or approved. Multiculturalism was, he urged

> *No sooner was the Cold War won than political scientist Samuel Huntington was prophesying that another, greater, conflict lay ahead in a grandiose battle between 'civilizations', especially one to be fought against 'Muslim fundamentalists'*

(reinvoking the terminology of the Cold War), 'basically an anti-Western ideology'. Spanish speakers in the south-west were threatening to fragment the USA linguistically, as were intellectuals critical of Americanization or of other expressions of American nationalism, and of the 'Anglo-Protestantism' that fundamentally sustained the national idea. The crisis was profound. As a conservative commentator glossed the case: 'The very unity and cohesiveness of the country are under siege, and the dominant trend – only "temporarily obscured" by Americans' response to the attacks of September 11 – is toward national disintegration.'[27] Rather than liberty and the American nation being naturally locked together, for followers of Huntington, Americans must steel themselves for war. The Patriot Act, pushed through in October 2001, despite its infringement of past freedoms, was applauded as the crucial bulwark of national identity. As Rudi Giuliani, ex-mayor of New York and a Republican presidential aspirant who is by no means an extreme conservative, put it:

I support the extension of the Patriot Act for one simple reason: Americans must use every legal and constitutional tool in their arsenal to fight terrorism and protect their lives and liberties. The attacks of September 11, 2001, made clear that the old rules no longer work. The terrorists who attacked us seek to kill innocent men, women and children of all races and creeds. They seek to destroy our liberties.[28]

A further complication in the present status of American nationalism lies in the debate over whether the world's super power is an empire and what that word might entail (thereby replaying the intermingling of nationalism and imperialism in nineteenth-century Europe). The secretary for defence in the Bush administrations, Donald Rumsfeld (resigned November 2006), has been anxious to deny the imperial title and instead fix it on the wicked 'empire-building Soviet Union' that was. Other conservative commentators have been less cautious, with one journalist maximizing his anti-liberal bile as he rejoiced that Americans were 'now coming out of the closet on the word empire'.[29]

Religion, national and Christian

For another group close to power during the Bush presidencies since 2001, the nation and empire must be revered in both this world and the next

For another group close to power during the Bush presidencies since 2001, the nation and empire must be revered in both this world and the next. The so-called 'Christian right' contains many currents, quite a few of which run counter to others. But for Pat Robertson, an evangelist who doubles as a political commentator: 'There will never be world peace until God's house and God's people are given their rightful place of leadership at the top of the world.'[30] The godly, he preaches, are likely to be American, although they will not all be Americans and it may be possible to locate virtuous people in other, similar, societies.

But it is the structural issue that is the most salutary feature of the spread of Christian fundamentalism in the USA. Even if the more rapturous adepts of this philosophy believe this world is destined soon to be destroyed in Christ's Second Coming, for the present they, too, accept the political form of the nation as a global given, just as, some isolationists apart, they applaud the world leadership role of the USA. Once likely to be anti-Semites of a banal kind, they now are fervent partisans of Zionist Israel, viewed as an accelerator of the coming rapture. Simultaneously their Americanism makes them anxious to improve and reform the nation at home. Their Christian beliefs and behaviour demand that they campaign against what they see as evil Enlightenment accretions to national holiness, typically wanting the teaching of 'intelligent design' to oust the 'un-Christian' and falsely rational scientific biology of Charles Darwin and the evolutionists. Like other nationalists, they look to history for justification, all the more since many Americans claim a Puritan birthright from first white settlement. In its advocacy of such policies and of a purer nation, the Christian right bids to fuse what it fears has become the inadequately passionate and crusading religion of the nation into a resurrected fundamentalist Christianity and label the amalgam the real national spirit of modern America. A newly godly USA, these zealots prophesy, will restore trust and unity to its citizens. The Christian god and the American god will become identical.

The case of Israel

This drift into marrying traditional religion with the religion of the nation is also evident, if in a different key, in the story of Zionist Israel and that of its Arab enemies (and of Hindu and other fundamentalists). To a degree, Israel is another 'new society', a settlement by Europeans in a world outside Europe, where there were, at least to the immigrants, 'vacant territories . . . without any locally entrenched encumbrances'.[31] Not titular Ottoman rule to 1918, or the British governing through League of Nations mandate, or local Arabs altered this conception for those Jews, assembling from more than 100 countries, who began to settle in the area.

Throughout its history, the Zionist movement has proven extremely factionalized; not all the Jewish arrivals at any stage of Israel's history were Zionists, but the country did have one major difference when compared with Australia and the USA. It did possess, or seem to possess, an ancient past. Jews, it could be proclaimed, were not really 'transplanted' to their nation state since its territory had always been theirs. This new society was simultaneously an old, even the oldest, nation, since 'Eretz Israel' (the land of Israel, with the term first appearing in the biblical Book of Samuel) was where independent 'national' Jewry was to be 're-founded'. The proclamation of a new nation state on 15 May 1948 was officially dated 'the fifth of Iyar 5708 by the Jewish calendar'.[32] David Ben-Gurion (1886–1973), destined to be the country's first key leader, had argued in 1926, when seeking to define his 'Labor Zionism': 'If it does not have the interests of the nation at heart and a sense of national destiny, a class cannot unite and impose its social and spiritual authority

on other classes of people.'[33]
The nation, he was pledging,
must outweigh any other factors in human identity.

The nation, he was pledging, must outweigh any other factors in human identity

The new nation began its existence as a parliamentary democracy and it has thereafter remained the only Middle Eastern country where free debate flourishes. Yet it was also born, politically and ideologically, with contradictions, practical and legal. British rule had been contested militarily. The fighters included the future prime minister Yitzhak Shamir and the terrorist 'Stern Gang', willing to use assassination as a political weapon. To the terror of the 'freedom fighter' was added war, in 1948–49, with the country's Egyptian and Arab neighbours and against those Palestinians, as they were coming to be known, who shared the territory to be ruled as Israel. In the first months of the new nation state's existence, some 800 000 Arabs fled from it or were expelled.[34] Thereafter, a sputtering of communal conflict continued and Israeli law prescribed that, although given the vote, the 20 per cent of the population who were Arab must stand outside the main processes of national development and remain relatively poor and deprived. Regular hostilities involving Arab states in 1956, 1967, 1973, 1982 and 2006 further ensured that Israel would become a militarized society where empathy was insistently nationalized.

Moreover, early legislation, which, although contested, has never been overthrown, maintained that Jews, no matter where they resided, had a special relationship with the 'land of Israel', one that was not shared by Arab Israelis, who could be citizens of the country but never possess full nationality. The country's flag drew on the Jewish prayer shawl for its design, the national emblem being the seven-branched candlestick that had graced the Temple destroyed by Roman emperors, Vespasian and Titus, in the first century AD, while the unofficial but regularly sung national anthem hailed Jews and only Jews. In 1950 Israel passed the so-called 'Law of Return', granting immigration rights and automatic nationality to any from 'the Diaspora' who wanted to settle there. Ben-Gurion proclaimed it the act that 'embodies the central purpose of our state'.[35] Arabs who had left in 1948, by contrast, were refused their right of return. Furthermore, the country's Education Law in 1953 demanded that pupils be inculcated with 'the values of Jewish culture'. Early talk about 'Judaizing' the surviving local Arabs and making Hebrew their language ceased.[36]

Then there was the Holocaust, as it became framed into so many countries' consciousness but especially into Jewish identity as the ultimate and unique, the ineffable, ethnic and racial horror. In 1980, the Holocaust was inscribed as a central event in the national history syllabus, being depicted in a way that separated it from any special context in the Second World War. Thereafter, it was stated, the Holocaust must be acknowledged as 'a defining moment for Israelis, an event that symbolized the Jews' uniqueness, their continuous victimization solely for the crime of being Jewish'.[37] The Holocaust was thereby thoroughly nationalized and its moral was that Jewish national life could 'never be normalized'.[38] As one non-Zionist Jew explained, the nation of Israel became a 'new old country [that] was uniquely old, uniquely new, uniquely victorious, and uniquely victimized'.[39] More contestably, it has been argued that, 'rather than representing a permanent escape from the ghetto, Israel became the ghetto's mirror image – an armed camp', one surrounded by a 'national' wall of its own construction that, in its pessimistic reading of the human condition, seemed a 're-ghettoization from within', deliberately designed to mock those who had innocently assumed that history was ending when the Berlin Wall was thrown down and that universal trust and happiness would thereafter ensue.

Militant but democratic Israel, in more critical view, 'the sole Western survivor . . . of the integral nationalism of interwar Europe in the postwar – and post-Cold War – world'[40], thus assumes a paradoxical place in the survival, and prospering under globalization, of the nation state. Here is a new country that does have more serious claims than most old countries to a long, even a long national, past. Here is a liberal democracy pledged to freedom that seems, always more in the national interest, to be obliged to limit or circumvent the liberal democratic ideals of the Enlightenment in its political acts. Once it was accepted that 'a liberal state can only be a secular state',[41] but Israel has never detached itself from identifying Jews by religious faith and commitment (even if at least half the population maintain that they are 'not religious'[42]). Here is a society where the heirs of those who suffered national, racial or religious persecution for so long cannot live in peace and amity with their neighbours or even with the non-Jewish segments of their own population. As one commentator described the situation: 'The common wish of virtually all Jews is that the Arabs would simply go away.'[43]

Short of catastrophe, the hope was, and is, vain and Israel seems destined to go on being an embattled nation in both practice and spirit, one where the dream of a modern nation state that can pass beyond narrow ethnicity and leave religion to individuals is very unlikely to come to pass. It is true that, for two decades,

> *Israel seems destined to go on being an embattled nation in both practice and spirit, one where the dream of a modern nation state that can pass beyond narrow ethnicity and leave religion to individuals is very unlikely to come to pass*

dissident historians have spoken up for the view that Israeli Jews were not only victims, and were not the only victims either, and have raised justified doubts about the seamless longevity and unity of Jewish identity through two millennia of the Diaspora. But they face critics from the right who denounce an intellectual conspiracy to impose 'post-Zionism' and 'post-Jewishness' on Jews and so dismantle the whole project of a Jewish nation.[44] The left fears instead that Israeli democracy is more and more challenged by a 'new messianism',[45] one that amalgamates the Jewish religion with the religion of the nation. Meanwhile, in much practice, the nation remains divided between those who are more or less religious Jews, between the heirs of the Ashkenazi and Sephardic traditions and between those with heritage in the rival past empires of Habsburgs, Hohenzollerns, Ottomans, Romanovs and the Soviets, or of the USA, as well as by the more common differences created by class and gender.

The nations against terror

The survival of vehement democratic debate is encouraging. Less so is the parallel that exists between the immigrant new nation, Israel, and such 'new societies' as the USA and Australia. In each, prompted by the 'war against terror' and the fearfulness of the present and seeming future, a populist nationalism gains ground and grows ever more strident and exclusionist. It is true that, in the USA and Australia, a narrowing definition of nationality is too contradictory to have full purchase in the real-world situation of an economic need for immigrants. Yet, perhaps in reaction to new arrivals with their potential expansion of the nation's histories, each country grows more jaundiced spiritually, with Australia adopting a populist assimilationism and the USA doing the same, while on the religious right there is an obstreperous emphasis on Christianity (of some definition) and the nation being made one. A pessimist might say that the view of contemporary Israel as the sole nation with a lingering fondness for integral nationalism is too confined; under the suzerainty of the globalizers, it may be back in business in many places.

> *A pessimist might say that the view of contemporary Israel as the sole nation with a lingering fondness for integral nationalism is too confined; under the suzerainty of the globalizers, it may be back in business in many places*

Nations in the wider world

This book is nearing its end. So far, however, its commentary has been decidedly Eurocentric, per force given that nations and nationalism came to the fore in nineteenth-century Europe. Even this chapter, in its surveying of contemporary developments in Australia, the USA and Israel, has concentrated on nations whose population in majority derived from Europe. Yet, the present United Nations (UN) boasts nearly 200 member states that run in size from tiny Pacific islands to the People's Republic of China, with a population well in excess of 1000 million. When the UN was founded, it had 51 members. The multiplication evident is yet another reminder of the difficulty of being too precise about the character, history and behaviour of nations. Most African states, for example, are new nations because decolonization occurred at a moment when the institution of the nation seemed the readiest and best replacement for imperial rule. Postcolonial history has proved unhappy for many because 'nation-building' in the region has hardly gone beyond the foundations, given the lingering power of 'tribal', personal, gender and other loyalties. Joseph Désirée Mobutu, one dictator among many, was the viciously corrupt ruler of the once Belgian Congo for a generation to 1997 and made typical attempts to nationalize his population by renaming the country Zaire, by according it a long history and by rooting its ideological base in African 'authenticity'. He also did some 'modernizing', and the country still boasts a mouldering nuclear power station. Yet, Mobutu never renounced his tribal connections, building a palace retreat in his homeland well upriver. The confusion of his policies, his rapacity and that of his friends and supporters, 'national' and international, ensured that the preaching about nationhood truly converted few citizens. In the post-Mobutu era, the Congo, as it is now renamed, like almost all African countries, remains scoured by many conflicts, a nation in little more than name.

In the Hispanic empire of Central and Latin America, nations were similarly beset by an ambiguous relationship with history. Each state was likely to contain the heirs of their sometimes European masters, of the inhabitants before white settlement (here there was opportunity for forging redolent pasts by evoking the allegedly spirituality of Aztec, Inca, Mayan or other 'first peoples'), of the slaves brought in by the global entrepreneurs of Britain, the Netherlands and other seafaring Europeans, and of the complex admixture of the three. Furthermore, by the twentieth century, each of the Hispanic states lived in the shadow of the US empire, to which they contributed migrants and natural wealth and from which they drew culture. The military dictatorships that long stained any hopes in social democracy in such places were the product of the jarring clash between nationalizing rhetoric and a broader political and economic reality.

In Central and Latin America, nations were similarly beset by an ambiguous relationship with history. Each state was likely to contain the heirs of their sometimes European masters, of the inhabitants before white settlement, of the slaves brought in by the global entrepreneurs and of the complex admixture of the three

But the most ambiguous 'nations' of the current world are to be found in the empire states of India, Iran, Ethiopia and China, and in the non-empire of the Arabs. It is these last who, if generally in the name of Palestinian nationalism but always with financial sponsorship and ideological encouragement from the Arab-speaking or Muslim religious world beyond Palestine, fight the latest *intifada* against the Jews and contest what they call the 'Israeli occupation' of 'their' land. Once again an integralist or worse devotion to blood and soil flourishes, and men and women and children kill and are killed for what they say is their nation. In practice, however, the Arab states are a mini-UN in their bewildering variety of size, constitutional structure, genuine mass base, level of modernization and domestic and foreign policies. Perhaps, as enthusiasts maintain, 'the bonds of Arabism are still important today',[46] but the divisions and contradictions are at least as significant. Indonesia and Pakistan (each a state arguably with as many claims to be an empire as a nation) are leading Muslim countries where the Koran has a powerful cultural role but where neither the ruling elites nor the population speak Arabic as their first language. Egypt is Arabic-speaking but forges its nation-justifying history around an ancient people who were not. The murders that are a daily occurrence in post-Saddam and post-Baathist Iraq are the products either of religious division between Sunni and Shia Muslims or of national division, with the Kurds being the most numerous people without a nation state in today's world.

The Baathists in Iraq, with an inheritance of a version of fascism from the French mandates in Syria and Lebanon, thought of themselves as modernizers and nationalizers,[47] although the pull of religion, tribalism, familism and the personality cult clouded matters. Osama Bin Laden and the philosophers of Al-Quaeda, by contrast, may seek the overthrow of the ruling dynasty in Saudi Arabia and flirt on occasion with Arabist enthusiasms, but their fundamentalism is religious in its framing, foreseeing an empire of the just, in the unlikely event of a global victory of their version of a Muslim utopia. For all their fervent desire to expel the Jews from an alleged Arab homeland, nationalism is too petty a matter to detain them long in their grandiose vision of the world. Although it contains flashes of nationalist rhetoric and can manipulate history in ways that nationalists pioneered, these fundamentalists are globalizers or nothing.

Perhaps the supremely paradoxical moment when it becomes plain that Osama, hiding from Stealth Bombers in some mountain cave and there maximizing in his dress and body language his antique purity, has something in common with the most insouciantly globalizing and modernizing capitalists in their joint allegiance to a version of universalism is a time to conclude this exploration of the meaning and fate of nationalism. As the third millennium wears on, war seems to have become sadly normalized in our world. Worse, so too does a cheerful acceptance of a deplorably enhanced intent in once liberal societies to curtail traditional liberties and infringe the rule of law and to justify this repression with the politics of fear. This blighting of the hopes in a world-ranging triumph of liberty, equality, fraternity and sorority sits uneasily with the spreading prosperity that has made citizens of the developed world unimaginably richer than they have been at any other time, and, however erratically, has begun to spread material contentment to other segments of the globe.

What remains a matter of debate is whether the success of the political form of the nation, certainly its cultural imprint on many peoples and perhaps its derivation from the populace, have helped humankind to progress over the past two centuries, despite the many premature deaths that have stained the history of every country in that time

What remains a matter of debate is whether the success of the political form of the nation, certainly its cultural imprint on many peoples and perhaps its derivation from the populace, have helped humankind to progress over the past two centuries, despite the many premature deaths that have stained the history of every country in that time. Did the economic advances, the unlocking of so many secrets by science, the expanding access to holiday and ease, occur in spite of the nations or because of them?

It is hard to respond confidently to queries about national virtue and achievement. Cleanliness, so the Victorians believed, is next to godliness and one popular yardstick by which national modernity is measured is the ability to control or conceal rubbish. In this as in so many other matters, the French led the way. In 1884, the deputy Eugène Poubelle pressed successfully for the availability of garbage bins in Paris and its environs and, in curious reward, they took his name. Thereafter a city was thought to be either in crisis or sadly backward if too many defecating dogs or piles of garbage polluted its streets. When the engineer–archaeologist Rodolfo Lanciani contemplated the task of excavating classical Rome after Italy took over government there from the Church, he was determined that the new nation must wipe clean the 'filth' of the past: 'I have never yet found an ancient building which did not conceal corpses – often only a few dozens, but sometimes millions', he remarked.[48]

If cleanliness remains a good thing in most eyes, the word 'cleansing' carries more negative overtones. Plans to alter the national makeup of a certain region, to homogenize and purify it, have a long history. In 1920 Benito Mussolini rejoiced at the prospect of the cleansing of Trieste – the purge, he thought, should eliminate both class enemies and those 'Slavs' (mainly, in fact, Slovenes) anxious to cling to a non-Italian identity.[49] Today, too, we are deluged with rhetoric urging that our country must above all be united and we should rally around the flag and anthem in nationally pious manner. Now, rather than 'alien' old inhabitants of the nation, the dangerous variety of difference is often seen to lie among newcomers, and states mimic each other in legislation designed to curb and diminish the survival of old immigrant histories in a new place of residence.

The force of the idea of national homogeneity is one of the great paradoxes of modern times, doubtless seconded by the inexorable spread of the industrial and technological revolutions with a natural-seeming narrowing of human variety, at least in regard to the most evident features of our identity. Science depends on rules, on regularity, on simplicity. One plus one (except for the most arcane) should always equal two. Therefore, it has seemed, in a modernized nation, everyone should speak the national language and obey its grammar and vocabulary. Too much variation leads to too much complexity and may foster contradiction, the breakdown of science, anarchy and worse.

The force of the idea of national homogeneity is one of the great paradoxes of modern times, doubtless seconded by the inexorable spread of the industrial and technological revolutions with a natural-seeming narrowing of human variety

Yet, everywhere and on all occasions, nostalgia for difference survives. Greens are anxious that no natural species should die out and great efforts are made to save those elements of nature that are under threat, while the DNA of departed species is treasured in the hope that they can one day be resurrected. Emphasis on human difference is more muted (except in regard to 'first peoples'; what was once damned as their 'primitiveness' is now frequently celebrated as healthy spirituality and wholesome nearness to the soil), with the nation often acting as a sort of destructive armed bulldozer wiping out knowledge of variety in the nation's past and trying to build a singular future on the resultant cleansed lot.

The thoughtless tyranny involved underlines the fact that the history of the nations is filled on the one hand with sacrifice and achievement and on the other with lies and horror. To tell the truth, nations certainly do not embody a united, holy and peaceful eternal people. Yet more universal solutions to the dilemma of administering humankind have not worked (and the European Union has scarcely eliminated, or aimed to eliminate, the national sense of people who are citizens of its component states). Similarly, pre-national societies, which still stud the developing world, are scarcely redoubts of human happiness. Maybe nations, like advertising, are a necessary falsehood. For the present, the best solution for each of us may be to pay our national taxes and enjoy our national citizenship but to resist those (and they are presently multiplying, despite their appalling role in the great crises of the Second World Wars) 'integral nationalists', who want the nation to provide the only and ultimate, the final, solution to all our troubles. A loyalty to the nation and a mellow sense of identity with it are fine, so long as its citizens do not allow their empathy with humankind, as with their

> *A loyalty to the nation and a mellow sense of identity with it are fine, so long as its citizens do not allow their empathy with humankind, as with their individuality and their class, gender, age, regional and other roots, to be nationalized as well*

individuality and their class, gender, age, regional and other roots, to be nationalized as well. If nationalism can only be permitted to remain banal, the lies at the heart of national history may work benignly and a crucial critical reading of the past by the nation's citizens can survive amid the jingoism. In any society, nations work best when they are limited to being a scarcely noticed base from which to cleave to the locality and simultaneously to explore the world. Humankind will defeat the creeping economic, religious, political and national fundamentalism of our times by clinging not to national but to humane values and the discipline of history will best second the process if it remains committed not to the nation but rather to democratic debate. Courteous and passionate argument without end remains the best counter to national final solutions.

Notes

1 L. Hartz (ed.), *The Founding of New Societies: Studies in the History of the United States, Latin America, South Africa, Canada, and Australia* (1964, New York: Harcourt, Brace and World), p. 4.

2 *Ibid.* p. 42.

3 R.N. Rosecrance, 'The radical culture of Australia', in Hartz, *The Founding of New Societies*, p. 311.

4 *Ibid.* p. 293.

5 R. Ward, *The Australian Legend* (1958, Melbourne: Oxford University Press).

6 W.K. Hancock, *Australia* (rev. edn) (1961, Brisbane: Jacaranda Press), pp. 24, 49, 59, 128, 218.

7 A.J. Grassby, 'Community relations means us all', in M. Bowen (ed.), *Australia 2000: The Ethnic Impact* (1977, Armidale: University of New England), p. 7.

8   R. Murri, 'Gl'Italiani nell'America Latina: impressioni di viaggio', *Nuova Antologia*, 1913, 1 April, f.991, p. 437.

9   A. Giordano, *Marco Polo . . . and After* (1974, Adelaide: A. Giordano), pp. 9, 13.

10 R. White, *Inventing Australia: Images and Identity 1688–1980* (1981, Sydney: George Allen and Unwin).

11 I. Clendinnen, *Dancing with Strangers* (2003, Melbourne: Text Publishing), p. 288.

12 B. Rossi, 'La Chiesa Cattolica e l'emigrazione', *Il Ponte*, 1974, 30, pp. 1587–8.

13 Hartz, *The Founding of New Societies*, p. 4.

14 M. Billig, *Banal Nationalism* (1995, London: Sage), pp. 50–51.

15 S. Terkel, *'The Good War': An Oral History of World War II* (1984, New York: Pantheon), p. 11.

16 J. Dower, *War Without Mercy: Race and Power in the Pacific War* (1986, New York: Pantheon), p. 33.

17 N. Ferguson, *Colossus: The Rise and Fall of the American Empire* (2004, London: Allen Lane), p. 209.

18 A. Haley, *Roots* (1976, New York: Dell Publishing).

19 E.U. Essien-Udom, *Black Nationalism: A Search for Identity in America* (1962, Chicago, IL: University of Chicago Press), p. vii.

20 N. Glazer, *Affirmative Discrimination: Ethnic Inequality and Public Policy* (1975, New York: Basic Books), p. 220.

21 P. Novick, *The Holocaust in American Life* (1999, Boston, MA: Houghton Mifflin), p. 114.

22 *Ibid.* pp. 146–69.

23 *Ibid.* p. 9.

24 *Ibid.* p. 171.

25 *Ibid.* p. 178.

26 See, initially, S.P. Huntington, 'The Clash of civilisations', *Foreign Affairs*, 1993, 72, pp. 22–49. The essay was widened into a book, *The Clash of Civilizations and the Remaking of the World Order* (1996, New York: Simon and Schuster).

27 See S.P. Huntington, *Who Are We? The Challenges to America's National Identity* (2004, New York: Simon and Schuster) and J.W. Caeser, 'The clash of the Huntingtons', *Weekly Standard*, 3 May 2004.

28 *New York Times*, 17 December 2005.

29 Cited by Ferguson, *Colossus*, pp. 3–5.

30 W. Martin, *With God on Our Side: The Rise of the Religious Right in America* (2005, New York: Broadway Books), p. 354.

31 D.J. Elazar, *Israel: Building a New Society* (1986, Bloomington, IN: Indian University Press), pp. 10, 13, 41.

32 Cited by Z. Sternhell, *The Founding Myths of Israel: Nationalism, Socialism, and the Making of the Jewust State* (1998, Princeton, NJ: Princeton University Press), p. 131.

33 *Ibid.*

34 J. Rose, *The Question of Zion* (2005, Princeton, NJ: Princeton University Press), p. 136.

35 Y. Hazony, *The Jewish State: The Struggle for Israel's Soul* (2000, New York: Basic Books), p. 56.

36 A. Dowty, *The Jewish State: A Century Later* (1998, Berkeley, CA: University of California Press), pp. 187–8.

37 D.A. Port, 'From the scandal to the Holocaust in Israeli education', *Journal of Contemporary History*, 2004, 39, p. 632.

38 *Ibid.* p. 633.

39 Y. Slezkine, *The Jewish Century* (2004, Princeton, NJ: Princeton University Press), p. 352.

40 *Ibid.* p. 364.

41 Sternhell, *The Founding Myths of Israel*, p. xiii.

42 Dowty, *The Jewish State*, p. 174.

43 Elazar, *Israel*, p. 167.

44 See, for example, Hazony, *The Jewish State*, p. xxiii.

45 Rose, *The Question of Zion*, p. 8.

46 R. Khalidi, 'The origins of Arab nationalism: introduction', in R. Khalidi et al. (eds), *The Origins of Arab Nationalism* (1991, New York: Columbia University Press), p. vii.

47 For (hostile) introduction, see S. Payne, *A History of Fascism, 1914–1945* (1995, Madison, WI: University of Wisconsin Press), pp. 516–17.

48 R. Lanciani, *Notes from Rome* (ed. A.L. Cubberly) (1988, Rome: British School at Rome), p. 17.

49 R.J.B. Bosworth, *Mussolini* (2002, London: Arnold), p. 149.

Short bibliography

The chapter endnotes of this book are its major guide to further reading but especially note the following:

Anderson, B. *Imagined Communities: Reflections on the Origin and Spread of Nationalism*, rev. edn (1991, London: Verso).

Armstrong, J.A. *Nations before Nationalism* (1982, Chapel Hill, NC: University of North Carolina Press).

Bell, P.M.H. *The Cult of the Nation in France: Inventing Nationalism, 1680–1800* (2001, Cambridge, MA: Harvard University Press).

Breuilly, J. *Nationalism and the State* (1993, Manchester: Manchester University Press).

Catherwood, C. *Why the Nations Rage* (1997, London: Hodder and Stoughton).

Cocks, J. *Passion and Paradox: Intellectuals Confront the National Question* (2002, Princeton, NJ: Princeton University Press).

Deutsch, K.W. *Nationalism and Social Communication: An Inquiry into the Foundations of Nationality*, rev. edn (1966, Cambridge, MA, MIT Press).

Deutscher, I. *The Unfinished Revolution: Russia 1917–1967* (1967, London: Oxford University Press).

Deutscher, I. *The Non-Jewish Jew and other Essays* (1968, Oxford: Oxford University Press).

Geary, P.J. *The Myth of Nations: The Medieval Origins of Europe* (2002, Princeton, NJ: Princeton University Press).

Gellner, E. *Thought and Change: The Nature of Human Society*
(1964, London: Weidenfeld and Nicolson).

Gellner, E. *Nations and Nationalism* (1983, New York:
Cornell University Press).

Gellner, E. *Encounters with Nationalism* (1995, Oxford: Basil Blackwell).

Hall, J. (ed.) *The State of the Nation: Ernest Gellner and the Theory of
Nationalism* (1998, Cambridge: Cambridge University Press).

Hastings, A. *The Construction of Nationhood: Ethnicity, Religion and
Nationalism* (1997, Cambridge: Cambridge University Press).

Hobsbawm, E. *Nations and Nationalism since 1780: Programme, Myth,
Reality* (1990, Cambridge: Cambridge University Press).

Hobsbawm, E. and Ranger, T. (eds) *The Invention of Tradition* (1983,
Cambridge: Cambridge University Press).

Hutchinson, J. and Smith, A.D. (eds) *Nationalism* (1994, Oxford:
Oxford University Press).

Ignatieff, M. *Blood and Belonging: Journeys into the New Nationalism*
(1993, London: Chatto and Windus).

Kedourie, E. *Nationalism* (1960, London: Hutchinson).

Kohn, H. *The Idea of Nationalism: A Study of its Origins and Background*
(1944, New York, Macmillan).

Kohn, H. *Prophets and Peoples: A Study of Nineteenth Century Nationalism*
(1947, New York: Macmillan).

Lawrence, P. *Nationalism: History and Theory* (2005, Harlow: Pearson
Education).

Mortimer, E. and Fine, R. (eds) *People, Nation and State: The Meaning
of Ethnicity and Nationalism* (1999, London: I.B. Tauris).

Mosse, G.L. *The Nationalization of the Masses: Political Symbolism and
Mass Movements from the Napoleonic Wars through the Third Reich* (1975,
New York: H. Fertig).

Ostler, N. *Empires of the Word: A Language History of the World*
(2005, London: Harper Collins).

Sahlins, P. *Boundaries: The Making of France and Spain in the Pyrenees* (1989, Berkeley, CA: University of California Press).

Slezkine, Y. *The Jewish Century* (2004, Princeton, NJ: Princeton University Press).

Smith, A.D. *Theories of Nationalism* (1971, London: Duckworth).

Smith, A.D. *The Ethnic Origins of Nations* (1986, Oxford: Basil Blackwell).

Smith, A.D. *National Identity* (1991, Harmondsworth: Penguin).

Smith, A.D. *Nations and Nationalism in a Global Era* (1995, Cambridge: Polity Press).

Suny, R.G. 'Constructing primordialism: old histories for new nations', *Journal of Modern History*, 2001, 73, 862–96.

West, L.A. (ed.) *Feminist Nationalism* (1997, New York: Routledge).

Woolf, S.J. (ed.) *Nationalism in Europe, 1815 to the Present: A Reader* (1996, London: Routledge).

Index

Adriatic 73, 106, 160

Aegean 50

Africa 46, 51, 85–6, 123, 169, 198

Ahmadinejad, Mahmoud 127

Ainu 119

Albania 123

Alexander the Great 29

Alexandria 32

Algeria 84

Alleghenies 15

Alps 16, 106

Alto Adige (South Tyrol) 106, 111

Anderson, Benedict 4–5, 112, 123

Annales 40–41

Anschluss 94, 111

anthropology 4, 49–50, 111, 140, 142–3

anti-Semitism 82, 89–95, 105, 113–15, 126–7, 144, 150–52, 155, 187–8, 191

Antonescu, Ion 115

Arabs 21, 91–2, 113, 126, 192–5, 199–200

Arctic Sea 142

Arthur, King 40

Atatürk, Kemal 92

Atlantic 143

Augustus, Emperor 11

Auschwitz 121, 123, 127, 151

Australia vii–ix, 3, 17–19, 23, 28, 30, 53, 85, 93, 125, 171–81, 192, 196–7

Austria (Austria-Hungary) 71, 74–5, 79–80, 84, 90, 93–4, 100, 106, 109, 111, 151, 158

Baldwin, Stanley 117

Bali 180

Balkans 16, 30, 51, 54, 77, 93, 100–101, 115, 158

Baltic Sea 15, 138

Bancroft, George 30

Barents Sea 140

Basques 15, 87, 116

Belgium 84, 109, 113, 198

Ben-Gurion, David 192–4

Berlin 32

Berlin, Congress of 77, 100

Berlin Wall viii, 195

Bessarabia 114

Bin Laden, Osama 200–201

Bismarck, Otto von 67, 77–80, 94

Blair, Tony 49
Blanc, Louis 72
bolshevism 6, 90, 110, 134–7, 139–40, 144, 147, 150, 153, 177
Bonn 176
Bosnia 100, 121, 158–9
Bourbons 25
Braudel, Fernand 40–42, 67
Brisbane 53
British Union of Fascists 117
Brittany 40, 57
Brutus 39
Bubrikh, D.V. 141
Bucharest 115
Buddha 143
Bukharin, Nikolai 136
Bulgaria 77
Burakumin 15, 119
Bush, George W. 182, 190
Byzantium 50

Calabria 24
California 4
Calley, William 56
calvinists 73
Cambodia 4
Cambridge 32, 112
Canada 21, 144, 181
Canberra 176, 179
capitalism 3, 5–6, 8, 10, 25, 32, 53, 71, 89, 113, 122–3, 134–5, 139, 152, 160–62, 168–9, 171, 181, 814–15, 201
Caporetto 106
Caracalla, Emperor 46
Carey, Henry 26
Carol, King 115

Carter, Jimmy 5, 185
Catalonia 15, 87, 116
catholicism 16, 17, 21, 37, 54, 65, 70, 76, 80, 106, 110, 116, 202
Caucasus 136, 149
Cavour, Camillo Benso di 72, 77–8, 80
Chad ix
Chartists 172
Chechnia 101, 149, 157
Chicago 87
China 4, 15, 17, 21, 24, 44–8, 52, 86, 116, 149, 169, 173, 198–9
Clark, C.M.H. ('Manning') 30, 175–7
Clendinnen, Inga 178
Cobbett, William 172
Cold War 110, 122, 134, 152, 171, 173, 185, 188–9, 195
Colley, Linda 57
Columbus, Christopher 186
communism vii, 32, 42, 48, 110, 112–13, 122, 136, 151, 154, 159, 161–2, 167, 171
Congo (Zaire) 198
Copenhagen 133
Cordoba 21
Cornwall 15
Corsica 68, 76
Cracow 151
Croatia 42–3, 90, 114, 121, 158–60
Cuoco, Vincenzo 74
Cyrenaica 89
Czech Republic (Czechoslovakia) 30, 90–92, 108, 111, 114, 117

Dacia 45
Danube 15
Danzig 111
Darlington 71
Darwin, Charles 177, 191
Demosthenes 30
Denmark 58, 79, 113
De Tocqueville, Alexis 176
De Troyes, Chrétien 40
Deutscher, Isaac 150–52
Dmowski, Roman 82–3
Dostoevsky, Fyodor 177
Drakulic, Slavenka 160–61
Dreyfus case 89

East Germany (DDR) 122
Economist, The 1, 5–6, 151
Edward I, King 13
Edward IV, King 59
Egypt 15, 17, 32, 193, 200
Eire 4, 15, 24, 57, 87, 113, 117, 174
Engels, Friedrich 67, 74, 141
England 13–14, 20–21, 24–5, 36, 38–9, 54–7, 87, 117–18, 133, 151, 172, 182
Enlightenment 7, 36, 44, 47, 53, 57–8, 64, 68–9, 76, 85, 87, 92, 95, 108, 124, 161, 169, 177, 191
Erasmus, Desiderius 36, 43–4
Erdogan, Tayyip 49
Eritrea 101
Estonia 108, 148–9
Ethiopia 15, 17, 24, 51–2, 86, 199
Etruscans 144
European Union 18, 125, 204

fascism 8, 22–3, 27–8, 76, 82, 91, 99, 106–8, 110, 112–13, 115–17, 121–3, 144, 158, 167
feminism 65
Fiji 101
Finland 113, 137–8, 140–41, 149
First World War 8, 11, 31, 77–8, 81, 93–4, 99–108, 110, 114, 124, 126, 158, 175
flags ix, 7, 10, 12, 25–6, 124, 193–4, 202
Flanders 11
France 12–13, 15, 20, 22, 24–8, 30–31, 37–8, 40, 42–3, 54–5, 57–8, 63–4, 66–8, 70, 72, 77–9, 84, 88–9, 101, 106, 108–9, 113, 132–3, 151, 158, 181, 200, 202
Francis Ferdinand, Archduke 100
Francis I, Emperor 74–5
Frankfurt 73–4
Freiburg 90
French Revolution 12, 25, 44, 55, 63–7, 70, 80, 88
Freud, Sigmund 90–94
Fukuyama, Francis 135
fundamentalism 33, 169, 191–2, 200, 205

Galicia 143
Gallipoli 180
Garibaldi, Giuseppe 93–4
Geelong 176
Gellner, Ernest 53, 111–13
Geneva 73, 109
Genghis Khan 48–9
Genoa 78
Geoffrey of Monmouth 30, 39–40

geography 14–19, 29, 44
Georgia 101, 136, 149
Germany 11, 15–16, 20, 22,
    30–31, 37, 43, 52, 56–8, 67,
    70, 73, 79–81, 83, 85–7, 90–92,
    95, 104, 106–7, 109–11, 114,
    116–18, 122–3, 125, 133, 140,
    144, 148–9, 151, 158–9, 181,
    187
Giordano, Antonio 175
Giuliani, Rudi 189–90
Glazer, Norman 185
globalization vii, 161, 168–71,
    195, 197, 200–201
Gobineau, Arthur de 88–9
Goebbels, Joseph 158
Goethe, Johann W. 68
Gogol, Nikolai 144
Gorbachev, Mikhail 154, 156
Goths 58
Gramsci, Antonio 6
Grassby, Al 173–4
Great Britain ix, 11–12, 15, 18–19,
    22, 25, 28, 30–32, 37, 39–40,
    43, 45, 56–7, 65, 84, 87, 89,
    106, 108, 113, 116–18, 123,
    125–6, 151, 158, 168, 172–4,
    176–8, 180–81, 192–3, 199
Greece 15, 21, 30, 37, 39, 43, 45,
    50, 73, 77, 91, 113, 122, 173
Guesdes, Jules 132–3
Gylling, Edward 140
Gypsies 52

Habsburg Empire 22, 32, 76, 79,
    81, 90, 92–5, 100–101, 144,
    157–8, 196

Hancock, Keith 172–3
Hannibal 90, 93–4
Hanson, Pauline 179
Harding, Warren 109
Hartz, Louis 172, 182
Helsinki 137
Henry V, King 38
Herder, Johann Gottfried von
    69–70
Hermannsdenkmal 80
Herodotus 45
Herzen, Alexander 73
Herzl, Theodor 94–5
Hindus 87, 192
Hiroshima 121
Hitler, Adolf 16–17, 84–5, 90,
    110–11, 113, 115, 122, 153
Hobsbawm, Eric 4, 31–3, 41,
    112–13
Hohenzollern dynasty 81, 101,
    196
Hollywood 186
Holocaust 1, 111, 121, 123–4,
    127, 187–8, 194
Homer 39
Horace (Q. Horatius Flaccus) 11
Hosking, Geoffrey 156
Howard, John 179–80
Hungary 22, 73, 75, 80, 90, 100,
    106, 109, 114, 151
Huns 144
Huntington, Samuel 188–9
Hussein, Saddam 200

immigration 7–8, 15, 18, 21–2, 24,
    42, 84, 168–70, 173–5, 178–82,
    184–6, 189, 196–7, 199, 203

imperialism 4, 47–8, 85–7,
119–20, 138–9, 181, 190
India 52, 86–7, 118, 169, 199
Indonesia 4, 200
Iran (Persia) ix, 15, 18, 42, 86–7,
127, 149, 199
Iraq 200
Irian Jaya 50
Irving, David 1
Israel (Jews) viii, 21–2, 24, 32–3,
37, 43–4, 51–3, 73, 90–95, 105,
107, 111, 113–15, 121, 123–7,
131, 135, 145, 149–55, 185–8,
191–7, 199–200
Istria 76
Italy vii–ix, 15–17, 20–24, 26–8,
31, 39, 43, 45, 57, 65, 67–8, 73,
78–9, 81, 84–7, 89, 92–3, 101,
103, 105–6, 109, 111, 116–18,
123, 159–60, 173–5, 186

Jacobins 65
Jakarta 4, 180
Jamaica 20
Japan ix, 15, 23–4, 48, 51, 86,
99, 109, 118–21, 125, 169, 173,
183
Jerusalem 52, 75, 91
Joan of Arc 66
John of Gaunt 14–15, 54
John Paul II, Pope 16–17

Kamenev, Lev 150
Karelia 137, 140–42
Kazantzakis, Nikos 15
Keynes, John Maynard 109
Khan, Mirza Malkom 87

Khrushchev, Nikita 141, 155
Kiev 143, 153, 156
Kipling, Rudyard 177
Kissinger, Henry 71
Kohn, Hans 91–2, 112
Kollontai, A.M. 133
Korea 15, 51, 86, 119, 149, 169
Kosovo 100–101, 127, 158
Kumming 4
Kurds 149, 200

Lanciani, Rodolfo 202
Latin America 198–9
Latvia 20, 108, 149
League of Nations 108, 192
Lebanon 200
Legion of the Archangel Michael
115
Leipzig 92
Lenin, Vladamir Ilych 109–10,
134, 136, 138, 141, 156, 161
Le Puy 65
liberalism 3, 6–7, 12, 63–4, 71–2,
76, 78, 94–5, 105–6, 108, 110,
113–14, 117–18, 122–3, 139,
157, 168, 172, 177, 182–3, 185,
189–90, 195, 201
Lithuania 108, 111
Livy (Titus Livius) 29, 45
Locke, John 182
Lollards 14
Lombroso, Cesare 107
London 32, 49, 77, 91, 94, 111–12,
118, 178
Louis XIV, King 26
Lueger, Karl 40, 93
Lulli, Giam Battista 26

lutherans 73
Lvov 144

Macedonia 123, 158
Malta 76
Ma'mins 51
Manchu dynasty 47
Manchuria 119
Maoris 101
Marx, Karl 67, 73–4, 141, 162
Marxism 4, 6, 8, 31–3, 41, 93, 112,
   116, 131–4, 142–3, 150–55,
   161, 169
Mayer, Arno J. 110
Mazower, Mark 50–51
Mazzini, Giuseppe 75–7
Mediterranean 41, 89, 173, 186
Medvedev, Roy 156
Meiji Restoration 118
Melbourne 176
Memel 111
Menzies, Robert 173
Metternich, Klemens von 71–2
Mexico 109
Michael, Tsar 104
Michelet, Jules 30, 41, 66–7, 177
Milosevic, Slobodan 160
Mobutu, Joseph 198
Moldavia 77
Moneta, E.T. 89
Mongolia 48–9
Montenegro 77, 158
Moravia 90
Morocco 116
Moscow 104, 146, 153, 156
Mosley, Oswald 117
Mosse, George 123–4

Murdoch, Rupert 169, 176, 180
Muslims 20, 43–4, 51, 54, 101,
   121, 123, 158–9, 189, 199–200
Mussolini, Benito 23, 25, 106,
   202
My Lai 56

Naples 74
Napoleon I, Emperor 56, 65,
   67–70, 85, 94
Napoleon III, Emperor 66–8, 73,
   79
Nazism 1, 8, 16–17, 41, 91–2, 94,
   99, 110–13, 116–17, 121–6,
   134, 141, 145–6, 149–51, 153,
   167, 173, 176, 187
Netherlands 36, 84, 113, 199
New Lanark 172
New York 178, 185, 189
New Zealand ix, 180
Nice 76
Nicholas II, Tsar 104, 131, 138,
   150
Nile river 15
NKVD 153
Nobel Prize 89
North Africa 15
Northumberland 55
Norway 20, 77, 113
Novick, Peter 127, 187
Nuremberg 124

Observer, The 151
Olympic Games 10, 180
One Nation 179
Ostler, Nicholas 20–21
Oxford 39, 186

Oxford English dictionary 13, 20
Oxford University Press 152
Owen, Wilfred 11–12

Pacific 15, 109, 143, 173
pacifism 89
Pakistan 15, 200
Palacky, Frantisek 30
Palestine 91, 126, 193, 199
Pamuk, Orhan 50
Papua New Guinea 17
Paraguay 21
Paris 25, 28, 37, 66, 73, 77, 91,
    100, 108, 111, 178, 202
Parti Ouvrier 132
Paul VI, Pope 181
Pearl Harbor 121
Pericles 30
Philip II, King 41
Picasso, Pablo 116
Piedmont 72, 78
Pilsudski, Joseph 151
Pitt, William 56–7
Pius VII, Pope 70
Pobedonostsev, Konstantin 150
Poland 15, 17, 73, 81–4, 99, 104,
    108, 114, 121–2, 138, 148, 151
Polo, Marco 175
Pol Pot 4
Po river 106
Porter, Brian 81–3
Portugal 15, 84
Poubelle, Eugène 202
Poujade, Pierre 179
Prague 91, 111–12
Princip, Gavrilo 100
Pristina 100

Prussia 67, 69–70, 79, 94
Pyrenees 15

Qajar dynasty 87
Queensland 179

racism 16, 87–95, 107, 111,
    118–22, 126, 128, 175, 178,
    183–4, 195
Ranger, Terence 32
Ranke, Leopold von 31
Reagan, Ronald 168
Renan, Ernest 12
Rhine 15
Rhineland 111
Richard I, King 38
Richard II, King 14, 38
Risorgimento 28
Robertson, Pat 190
Rocco, Alfredo 106–7
Roman Empire 11, 15, 21, 24, 30,
    40–41, 44–7, 49, 52, 58, 81, 194
Romania 45, 77, 114–15
Romanov dynasty 81, 87, 101,
    103–5, 134, 137–8, 143, 145,
    150, 196
Romanticism 15, 18, 75
Rome 23, 29, 37, 43, 90, 107, 116,
    144, 202
Roosevelt, Franklin Delano 120
Rousseau, Jean-Jacques 58
Rumsfeld, Donald 190
Russia 15, 17, 20, 23, 31, 53, 55,
    73, 79, 84, 89, 99, 103–8, 114,
    131, 133–4, 136–7, 141–2,
    144–7, 149–50, 155–6, 158, 177
Ruthenia 90, 122

Sahara 52

Sahel 52

St Helena 70

St Petersburg (Petrograd, Leningrad) 134–5, 137

Samarkand 48

Sarajevo 100

Saudi Arabia 200

Savoy dynasty 101

Schönerer, Georg von 94

Scotland 13, 15, 37, 43, 56–7, 87, 117

Scott, Walter 66

Second World War 4, 8, 41, 78, 101, 110, 115, 119, 122–3, 127–8, 141, 147, 149, 153–4, 156–8, 173, 182–3, 186, 194, 204

Seneca (Lucius Annaeus Seneca) 21

Senegal 101

Serbia 73, 77, 86, 90, 100–101, 121–2, 127, 158–60

Severan dynasty 46

Shakespeare, William 14, 102

Shamir, Yizhak 193

Sibelius, Jean 137

Singapore 19

Skrypnyk, Mykola 146

Slezkine, Yuri 51–2

Slovakia 114

Slovenia 22, 121, 158–60, 202

Smith, Adam 162

Smith, Anthony D. 112

Social Darwinism 20, 82

socialism 25, 64, 72, 79, 89, 106–7, 113, 132–5, 138–9, 145, 148, 150, 156, 169, 172, 199

Solzhenitsyn, Alexander 155

Somalia 51, 101

Soros, George 112

South Australia 175

Spain 21, 37, 51, 54, 84, 87, 115–16, 136, 189, 199

sport 6, 10, 12, 23, 89, 120

Stalin, Joseph 113, 116, 126, 135–8, 141–3, 145, 147, 149, 151–4, 156–7

Stargardt, Nick 125

Stephen, King 39

Stockton 71

Sudan 52, 200

Sudetenland 111

'Svevo, Italo' 22

Sweden 20, 113

Switzerland 58

Sydney 177

Syria 46, 200

Tacitus (P. Cornelius Tacitus) 45

Tamurlane (Timur the Lame) 48–9

Taylor, A.J.P. 117

terrorism viii, 75, 158, 169–70, 190, 193, 196

Thailand 4

Thatcher, Margaret 168

Thessaloniki (Salonica) 50–51

Thompson, Edward P. 57

Ticino 76

'Tito' (Josef Broz) 157–8, 160

Titus, Emperor 194

Tokyo 119

totalitarianism 22–3, 75, 106, 122, 167

Treblinka 124, 127
Trentino 106
Trieste 16, 73, 202
Tripolitania 89
Trotsky, Leon 131–2, 135, 150–52
Troy 39–40, 143
Turin 70, 77
Turkey 37, 44, 49–50, 54, 77, 80,
    89, 92, 100, 126, 180, 192, 196

Ukraine 122, 137, 143–7, 155–6
Ulaanbaatar 49
United Nations 101, 197–9
USA ix, 4–5, 15, 17–18, 24, 26,
    30–31, 56, 66–7, 71, 89, 91–3,
    108–10, 118, 120, 123, 125,
    139, 144, 149, 154, 168, 172–3,
    182, 192, 196–7, 199
USSR 3–4, 8, 20, 22–3, 28, 113,
    116, 121–2, 125, 134–56,
    158–9, 161, 167, 176, 190, 196
Ustasha 121, 158
Uzbekistan 48

Venice 37, 43, 106, 175
Verdi, Giuseppe 75
Versailles, Treaty of 100, 110, 113
Vespasian, Emperor 194
Victor Emmanuel I, King 71
Vienna 32, 90, 92–3, 144
Vietnam 4, 26, 56, 71, 86, 94, 101,
    185
Virgil (Publius Vergilius Maro)
    39

Vivekansada, Swami 86–7
Voltaire, (François-Marie Arouet)
    58

Wales 11–13, 15, 39–40, 56–7,
    87, 117
Wallachia 77
Ward, Russel 172
Warsaw 151
Western Australia 17
West Indies 15
whiggery 29
White, Richard 177
Wilhelm II, Kaiser 79
Wilson, Woodrow 69, 100,
    108–10, 121, 161, 167
Wisconsin 123
Wollstonecraft, Mary 65
women 8, 36, 46, 64–5, 75, 162,
    177, 196
Wyclif, John 13

Yemen 21
Yugoslavia 42, 109, 114, 121–2,
    135, 157–61
Yunnan 4

Zevi, Sabbatai 51
Zhirinovsky, Vladimir 157
Zimbabwe 86
Zinoviev, Grigorii 136, 150
zionism 24, 32–3, 44, 91–2, 94–5,
    113, 126, 150, 152, 187, 191–2,
    194, 196